Jean Phillips-Martinsson

Swedes
As Others See Them

Facts, Myths or a Communication Complex?

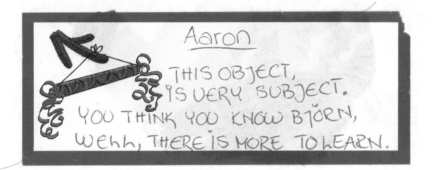

Aaron

THIS OBJECT,
IS VERY SUBJECT.
YOU THINK YOU KNOW BJÖRN,
WELL, THERE IS MORE TO LEARN.

Till Aaron

från Anna o Micke

Julen -91.

Studentlitteratur

Backcover photograph: Ulf Karlsson
Illustrations: Riber Hansson

ISBN 91-44-20112-5 Studentlitteratur
© Jean Phillips-Martinsson and Studentlitteratur 1991
Second Edition
Printed in Sweden
Studentlitteratur, Lund

Printing:	1	2	3	4	5	6	7	8	9	10	1995	94	93	92	91

Contents

To all Swedish citizens who work internationally including those who, like my husband, have had the good taste to marry foreigners and so enrich the Swedish society!

And to the ever-growing number of foreigners who have dealings with the Swedes through subsidiaries, joint-ventures, acquisitions or international projects.

Foreword

The importance of personal relationships in international business should not be underestimated. In my capacity as the door-opener for Swedish export delegations, I am constantly reminded of this.

The fact that others often conduct their business and social lives differently from that to which we are accustomed in Sweden, is a challenge to our flexibility! But understanding and respect for these cultural differences, and the willingness to learn from them, are key factors for success on world markets.

I have found Jean Phillips-Martinsson's book on these issues very valuable and have enjoyed reading it.

Bertil
Prince of Sweden

Introduction

This is an update. The English version, published first in 1981, has sold in over 40,000 copies and my publishers have been rubbing their hands with glee and gently prodding me to update. But have the Swedes themselves changed that radically during the last ten years?

Are peoples' basic norms, values, attitudes, priorities, expectations, customs, traditions and behaviour affected, in fact, by world events and changes in the society? I think not.

That the traumatic death of Prime Minister Olof Palme cruelly awakened the Swedes from their cocoon of security woven for them by the Welfare State, there is no doubt. The fact too that immigrants have made Sweden into a multicultural country with all that that implies, and that students have the chance to study abroad and travel inter-rail hopefully widens our horizons. But Swedes will still speak, think and behave like Swedes. A nation's basic cultural norms and values do not change significantly, due to external factors. For instance, at Swedish universities it is still foreign students who ask the most questions and enter into hot discussions!

What *has* changed is the interest shown in this field. It may be partly due to the fact that satellite communication has brought the dramatic global events of the last few years into our homes. News from every corner of the globe makes its way into our living rooms.

In 1975, there was practically no Swedish research to which I could refer, and I had no colleagues whatsoever in Europe. To-day, thanks to researchers like Åke Daun, Professor in Ethnology, we practitioners have some theories[1]! And there is an ever-growing worldwide network of intercultural consultants.

When the first edition of this book was published, I anticipated flowers and champagne, or even rotten eggs. I did not expect the deathly silence which ensued when 190 Swedish friends and clients received their free copies. No slaps on the back, no hugs and kisses – in fact, no spontaneous reaction whatsoever for two whole weeks.

Then, God bless him, the King of Sweden returned from a visit to Saudi Arabia. At a gathering of businessmen he stressed the importance of understanding the Arab mind, customs and traditions. The TV reporter, commenting on this, then linked His Majesty's message with that in my book. Overnight my book and I became public property!

Previously, I had considered myself to be a serious consultant with long-term contracts with my clients. Suddenly I was drowned by invitations from government, industry, educational and charity organisations wanting me to give them a 'quick fix'. Newspaper reporters and radio producers fell over themselves to interview me. One of my clients showed his appreciation at last by sending me – not flowers and champagne – but a pot of facial cream for 'tired, withered skins'!

Even the other day, in fact, an eminent organisation asked me to lecture to a group of top American executives. They had specifically asked to be briefed on the cultures of all the EC countries, Japan and the Arab States. I was to be given 20 minutes. I declined!

However, every cloud has a silver lining. 40,000 copies is a lot of books in such a narrow field. The growing interest and acceptance of the importance of the field is reward enough. So who buys it and what do they do with it?

Swedish companies order it for their employees, and for their foreign subsidiaries and customers. Politicians, embassy staff and those who represent Sweden abroad hope to discover which Swedish communication styles can be exported and which can best be left at home. Universities have it as compulsory or recommended reading and use it in their business, technical, economic and international studies. Language teachers use it as an extension of language, and the Swedish version is used mainly by small-sized companies, in immigrants' Swedish classes, in Scandinavian studies at foreign universities and by Mr. and Mrs. Svensson.

Another example of its use. One of my clients complained that they had just acquired a 'ghastly new boss' – a Swede who had spent several years in the US. They described him as follows:

> *He behaves like a child – loses his temper, shouts, goes red in the face and then guffaws. It may be OK behaviour in the States, but it certainly won't wash here!*

10 days later, the boss himself phoned me. He told me that he would like to meet me as no less than five of his employees had given him my book! We met and this is what he had to say:

> *I can't stand the slow pace, the quiet insolence with which my staff greet my outbursts! I hear myself talking too much and laughing too loud, but I can't help myself. It is driving me crazy!*

A couple of years later, he and his family moved to the UK where 'the boss' is still able to throw his weight about more than is acceptable in Sweden.

Not better, nor worse – just different!

Jean Phillips-Martinsson
Stockholm

The Cross-Cultural Perspective

In the following pages we shall be looking at how the Swedish businessman fares out in the world through a *cross-cultural* perspective. We shall be studying how he judges himself, how he is judged by his trading partners and subsidiaries and how he judges them. We shall also be examining some of the effects of these judgements.

For ease of reading I shall be using the term 'business*men*' to cover both men and women. *Business person* is a loathsome concoction and reduces us all to the state of robots. Let's face it, we women are all too little represented in the international business world. It is high time that our qualities were recognised as often being highly suitable for such work on many markets. Our global acceptance will obviously take many years, and maybe by then a suitable term will have been conceived!

We must bear in mind that how one person experiences another is determined not merely by the other's behaviour, but by the values, expectations and personality of the perceiver. People will therefore interpret the same situation differently.

Take a Swede, when he regards his business behaviour as appropriately 'cautious', it may be judged and misinterpreted by others as 'indecisiveness'. Many Latins will consider the Swede 'uncommunicative' due to his relatively silent behaviour. The Swedes, on the other hand, often consider Latins to be bad communicators, due just to their verbal capacity and apparent lack of listening ability!

But if the Swedish businessman gives the impression of being one of these 'uncommunicative' people, it becomes unimportant to discuss whether it is true or not since people *are* judged by the impressions they make. What is important is to discover if they have any negative effects on Sweden's international relations, what lies behind them, if anything can be done about them and if so, what?

Just as we all have preconceived ideas about what Frenchmen, Americans, Japanese or Arabs are like, so have they stereotyped notions about us. But we rarely recognise our own stereotypes! Often the impressions made by one individual are enough to make these stereotypes stick. It is up to each of us to ascertain then that the impressions we make on others are those that we intend to make.

Many excellent books have been written by anthropologists and sociologists which take up the problems of adjustment (culture shock) to living and working abroad *in general*. But few have been written expressly for the Swedish businessman whose job takes him from one country to the other. This book is intended to fill that gap and to help his trading partners and subsidiaries understand him better. Although it is written in an easy-to-read, humoristic manner, it is hoped that the communication problems it illuminates will not be taken lightly.

In Chapter 1 we discuss the importance of cultural awareness. What does it imply? We also take up the taboo question of national characteristics. *Is* there something specific about the Swedes that is 'typically Swedish'? How do they see themselves and how do others see them? Chapter 2 relates some of my own impressions and experiences when I first came to live in Sweden 30 years ago. I want to share them with you because even today they are identical to those experienced by many foreign visitors and immigrants who come to Sweden speaking no Swedish and having no knowledge of Swedish ways. First impressions are very potent and foreign businessmen rarely have the time to stay long enough to obliterate them completely.

In Chapter 3 we look at some facts and myths about Sweden and the Swedes. Is the Swedish model dead? In Chapter 4 we study the foreign businessmen's impressions of the Swedes, based on interviews with them. In Chapter 5, what causes some of these impressions. Chapter 6 discusses management styles and looks at some of the comparative research undertaken as regards Swedish management styles. Chapter 7 gives advice to Swedes on how to communicate better with their foreign counterparts and will, I hope, be appreciated by foreign readers! But communication is a complex business and to generate good cross-cultural relations, *both* parties must pull their weight, and learn to understand and respect one another. So Chapter 8 gives advice to foreigners and will, I am sure, be appreciated by the Swedes!

'Swedes As Others See Them', unlike many books written by foreigners about the Swedes, is not an attack on them and their system. On the contrary, my hope is that it may help explain what sparks off these myths of uncommunicative people with no 'joie de vivre', living in a 'smörgåsbord full of economic and social problems', as the French paper 'Le Monde' put it, and add something to the current Internationalisation and Quality of Life Debates.

1 Cultural Awareness Can Bring Home the Contract

This book is intended to be a thought-provoker and a basis for discussion. Its aim is to impress upon those working internationally the increasingly important role which people's cultural backgrounds play in the decision-making process and in the success or failure of enterprises.

It is often people who compete to bring home the contract, rather than nations, companies or products. People whose culture influences them to think and act according to the norms prevalent in their own countries. That means that, products and terms being equal, the potential buyer will quite simply choose the partner whom he likes best. He will choose the one he trusts. The one with whom he can build a rapport.

If an export manager sent out by his company cannot communicate on the business *and* social level with the foreign customer, and has no respect for the different ways of conducting business and behaving socially, the customer may well choose another partner. Negotiating with foreigners requires far more tolerance, awareness, sensitivity and flexibility than on the home market.

Neither is the *buyer* invulnerable in world markets today when unforeseen circumstances such as the oil crisis, shortages of raw materials, under-capacity in production or strikes rear their ugly heads. Whether or not he receives his order may well depend on the personal relationships which he has built up with his supplier.

Transnational acquisitions, joint-ventures and mergers are becoming daily news on world stock markets. But what happens to *people* in these new partnerships? Studies show that a large percentage of these marriages fail and end up in the divorce courts, often due to the incompatibility of the parties concerned.

The Social Democratic government's delay in applying for EC membership, has forced Swedish companies to set up production within the Community which accounts for half of the Swedish exports. In the first half of 1990, Swedish enterprises launched 125 corporate raids in Europe – the largest foreign investment in the continent last year by any nation, including US and Japan. Many have chosen *The Swedish Way* of cohabitation before taking the plunge into marriage, but rarely without upheavals.

Before choosing a partner, companies should undertake a 'cultural mapping'. This means that they should look, not just at the profit picture and technological advantages, but at the *human resources* they will be acquiring. Everyone in the organisations concerned will be affected in some way by the merger of two different business cultures and should, without delay, be prepared to meet and cope with them.

Being flexible enough to allow market conditions to guide us and to know when to accept others' ways of doing things, without losing sight of our own identity, is no easy task. To achieve it, the Swedish businessman must become more aware of his own culturally influenced patterns of behaviour – his 'Swedishness' – and take a good look at himself as others see him. So let's do that!

I have never met a people so prone to self-criticism, and yet so nationalistic as the Swedes: 'Vi är alla torrbollar', literally translated, 'We are all dry balls!' This description would hardly seem appropriate when studying their behaviour at international sports events! Should the Swedish team or individual not win, the TV commentator will always console the nation by reminding them that the winners had some historical connection with Sweden!

As far as self-criticism is concerned, not just do they unanimously admit to having a very special communication problem – and then refer negatively to themselves as being 'typically Swedish' – but their complex is magnified by wide support given to it in the mass-media.

During my years in Sweden I became sick and tired of assisting at the dissection of the Swede. Everyone analysed the situation, found excuses for it, but nobody *did* anything about it. So I decided to give it a try.

My specific field of interest has been just the Swedish businessman. After all it is he, with his international contacts, who is acting ambassador for Sweden and can do so much to make or mar the Swedish reputation. Since 1975, I have trained some 10,000 managers in cultural self-awareness and in the art of projecting themselves appropriately on the respective markets. And while learning about themselves, they automatically learn about others.

With a grant received from the Swedish Trade Council, I inter-viewed 171 foreign businessmen from many different countries to discover how the Swedish businessman is rated out in the world. Those interviewed were encouraged to give their spontaneous reactions to communication problems encountered with their Swedish counterparts.

In brief, the Swedish businessman was regarded as *inflexible in his negotiations and behaviour – unwilling to discuss and adjust, slow to make decisions, avoids conflict, over-cautious, and a stickler for punctuality. Difficult to get to know, hard to work with and for, stiff, no fun, dull and conceited.*

I am sorry to tell you that this description still holds good! It is confirmed by studies undertaken with foreigners from multi-nationals, by Swedish foreign subsidiaries during my workshops and by other independent studies. Naturally, they have many lovely things to say about you too, but since those don't cause problems, they are not forthcoming.

In defense of the Swedes, let me repeat that I was asking for the communication *problems* encountered. Had I asked similar questions about the British, Frenchmen, Americans – even Norwegians – the results would surely have been equally negative, but different! So to the question 'Surely we are no worse than the Norwegians or the Finns?', I reply that this is *not* intended to be a comparison study. Others' behaviour is not better or worse, right or wrong – just different.

Cultural Self-Awareness

National characteristics exist! There I have said it and stuck my neck out in a country where to do so is inadvisable – according to the Swedes' own self-analysis. During the 80's there has been a noticeable increase in studies undertaken on the subject and in the literature published.

But national characteristics, sometimes referred to as *stereotypes,* do not describe *individuals,* but merely the behavourial norms of a particular group. Within each group there are, of course, several exceptions to the norm, but individual exceptions are never as pronounced.

Stereotypes thrive when nations work together – sometimes they are cruel and others illustrate a love/hate relationship. But the fact that they continue to thrive gives them some historical interest. How about the British/American ones from the 2nd World War? The Brits were referred to as 'Limeys' by the Yanks. 'Limeys' to the Americans were pasty-faced, undernourished individuals who spoke in silly voices and had silly helmets. They were cheerful, cocky creatures whom the lusty, gum-chewing, gung-ho Yank found entirely impossible to understand. To the Limey, the Yank was overpaid, oversexed and over here! My guess is that many more will stem from the war in the Persian Gulf and, although nobody will take them terribly seriously, they will make their impact and go down in history.

Studies have shown that we are blind to our own culture. Yet, to work successfully with and for people from other cultures, we need first to understand our own culture. That is why, for the past 17 years. I have been working with my clients and collecting data on their national characteristics. Having done this, it is easier to compare them with others, in order to discover where their similarities and differences may lie. They make fascinating reading, so let's look at some of the Swedish ones!

Swedish National Characteristics

Swedish businessmen describe themselves as being:

organised	*loyal*	*polite*
reliable	*correct*	*private*
effective	*serious*	*highly educated*
rational	*punctual*	*diplomatic*
structured	*controlled*	*'lagom'*
honest	*calm*	*equal*
ethical	*quiet*	*conformists*

Most of these qualifications are considered positive by the Swedes because they describe the behaviour expected of them, according to their value system. But they are also very *self-critical* and well aware that just these same qualifications can make them :

inflexible, over-cautious, unsociable, narrow-minded, shy, conceited, stiff, jealous and scared of making fools of themselves.

In fact, just those things that foreigners complain about, as you will see in Chapter 4.

Let's take *highly educated*. The Swede means by this that he has a good all-round general education; often goes on to further education; reads more newspapers per capita and has more trade and technical magazines than most other nations. In others' eyes and ears, this can make him appear arrogant and conceited. In countries where

Culture with a capital C is given pride of place, the Swede, on the contrary, is considered *uneducated!*

'I've rarely met a Swede who can discuss music, literature, poetry or art', is the exclamation made by people from countries who value a classical education, rather than a technical one.

Lagom is a word which few Swedes can do without. It is the Swedish way of *conforming* to the unwritten rules of society – not to stand out. One should not talk too much, nor laugh too loud. In fact, it is safest to keep *quiet*, cool, *calm* and collected at all times. Neither should one risk losing face by disagreeing in public, nor sticking one's neck out! Their political policies of non-alignment are *lagom* too – to be, or not to be – the middle way. In other words, one should be *diplomatic and sit on the fence*. This behaviour will, in turn, be perceived as *over-cautious, narrow-mindedness and as trying to avoid conflict* or, in case of war, 'letting others do your dirty work for you'.

According to Åke Daun's studies, the *private* Swede likes nothing more than to get away from the maddening crowd by taking long lonely strolls in the woods. He is comfortable with his own company, because he then has no cause to adapt his ways to others, no reason to blot his copy book and no need to make boring chit-chat![1]

When a Swede is *well-organised, effective and punctual*, he considers that he is fulfilling his moral obligation and 'doing his share'. Others sometimes describe him as a 'workoholic!'

In Swedish eyes, being *honest* means telling the truth and keeping your word. This means that he is unlikely to give compliments as, in his eyes, it would be an exaggeration of the truth. Have you ever heard a Swede say something like 'May I congratualate you on your beautiful wife?' or to a colleague 'What a fantastic job you made of that project!' Telling stories is not usually the forté of such an honest person, since good story-tellers don't have to stick to the truth. It is more important to catch and keep your audience.

'There were only about *ten* persons there, not *hundreds* as you claimed'. Death to any spontaneous story-teller! Others consider the Swede *dishonest* because 'he's not direct – never says what he thinks!'

Egalitarianism has been one of the dominant social themes in Sweden where the gaps between people's living standards are unusually narrow – there are no slums and comparatively few mansions. All people are meant to have equal rights. What is yours, should and could be mine! Competition is not considered respectable and is discouraged. Some say that the *Swedish jealousy* thrives on such a system; others that it fosters the system.

When I compare these national characteristics with those from other nations which I have collected, it is incredible how similar the Dutch ones are to the Swedish. The main exception being that the Dutch *are* direct and usually say exactly what they think!

Although stereotypes can be questionable, used intelligently they can give you a lot of help. Studies show, in fact, that there is a lot of truth in them – even if we rarely appreciate our own stereotype!

2 First Impressions

As human beings we all have different roles to play in life, in our private lives and in our public lives – as individuals, spouses or parents, and as managers or subordinates. In Sweden, as in many other western countries, public and private lives are kept apart. Whereas in many other parts of the world, the two are inseparable. This is one of the many cultural differences to which Swedes living and working abroad need to adapt. The trouble is that when they do, they generally enjoy it so much that they do not return!

Many foreigners who come to Sweden expect to make friends with their business acquaintances. Others come to make initial contacts, build up a friendship and anticipate that the friendship will result in mutually profitable business transactions. First impressions are vitally important to them and often determine the success or failure of their missions. What is more, they take these impressions home with them to their countries and others are influenced by them.

Like all visitors to foreign countries, they have to learn the way of life – the unwritten rules of business and social behaviour. They have to learn how to make contacts, and not necessarily to set about it, as I did, in the same way they would at home. They have to find a common language with which to communicate, to understand the different timing system – how to make and keep appointments – the entertaining and eating habits and so on.

That is why I shall be sharing with you in the following pages my own professional and private experiences in these respects. Maybe they will help the Swedes to be better equipped to understand and deal with the 'culture shock' experienced by many foreigners, and help foreigners to avoid some of the pitfalls.

Professional

My first professional encounter with the Swedes was in 1952 at the Organisation for Economic Co-operation and Development (OECD) in Paris. International organisations are a culture unto themselves and should perhaps be described as 'sub-cultures' and OECD was no exception – a sub-culture with Paris outside. Even amongst diplomats, who have every reason to be cosmopolitans, one could distinguish cultural traits. Accordingly, we had nicknames for all delegations and the Swedish delegation was nicknamed 'The Quiet Men' – they *attended* meetings, yes, but rarely *participated*. They arrived punctually, were always very polite and well-dressed, but stuck together and rarely opened their mouths!

Some 10 years later I went to work and live in Sweden. Employed by a Swedish advertising agency as their international public relations consultant, I assisted in negotiations to sell a campaign to an English and an American client. It was during these negotiations that the need for this book became apparent to me.

Technically the campaign was impressive and weeks of work had gone into it, but its presentation left much to be desired. There was no aggressiveness, no counter-arguments. Only a passive resignation, or silence to all proposals made by the client giving the impression that agreement had been reached. Yet neither Americans nor Englishmen are particularly impressed by 'yes men'...

It was perhaps the fact that the Swedes understood and spoke such good English that misled the client into assuming that they also discerned all the motives behind their reactions. But fluency in a language is no guarantee of *cultural literacy* – an understanding of the differences in such things as attitudes, customs and behaviour.

For instance, the Swedes got straight down to business with no 'small-talk'. When I attacked them after the meeting for their bad manners, their excuse was, 'We have seven times as few people in our country as in yours and therefore we have to be seven times more effective. We have no time for such trivialities.' I'm still trying to work out the logic of this argument! Suffice to say that in their struggle to be productive and efficient, they totally ignored the vital importance of personal relations.

Similarly, many proposals put by the Americans and Englishmen showed a total lack of knowledge on their part about cultural differences affecting the Swedish market. Unaware of the differences themselves, the Swedes had a hard time defending their own proposals.

Having worked closely with all three nationalities involved, I was able to anticipate the pitfalls and found myself acting as an interpreter of cultural patterns of behaviour, rather than of language.

Since many of my colleagues preferred to go home to their families, television and glass of beer, I often had the pleasant task of entertaining the foreign guests. As we foreigners left the 'foreign territory' of the Swedish office one of them would invariably explode, 'Gosh! How do you stand them? They are so heavy-going.' This recurrent remark confirmed my opinion that the communication problem experienced by the Swedes was even more accentuated in international business. They are always obliged to negotiate in a foreign language which makes it even more difficult to project their personalities.

I had been warned not to expect any socialising with my colleagues after office hours as I hade been used to in the OECD and the pub life of London. However, I arrived in June after the start of the school holidays, and was agreeably surprised to find so many

Family pets are shipped off to the islands on holiday.

'bachelors' with nothing to do after office hours but to show me the sights and wine and dine me in restaurants. It was soon explained to me that wives, children, dogs, cats, Guinea pigs, hamsters, parrots and all the other family pets were shipped off to their various country homes, placed often on one of the many thousands of islands dotted around Sweden's coast.

But by the end of August when all the families returned to town, the warning held true. It took two years for one of my colleagues to invite me home to meet the family! When asked by his wife why he had waited so long, he replied, 'Firstly, Jean didn't speak Swedish and I thought you would be embarassed to speak English in front of me. Secondly, I wanted to get to know her to be sure she'd fit in with the family!'

I can hear many of you muttering: 'That wasn't the real reason. It is simply the fate of a single girl arriving in a foreign country and a jealous wife. It happens all over the world.' I do not agree. Many of my friends – married couples, bachelors and spinsters – have had the same experience. Neither do many countries have these long summer vacations, when the breadwinner is left to his own devices. He feels lonely too, hates going home to make his own food in an empty house and is delighted to have company in the restaurant – male or female. When the family returns, life gets back to normal. Swedish families, as many others, are inclined to have an established small circle of friends and hesitate to enlarge it. What is more, many wives work full-time and are too tired to start cleaning the house and making a meal. It is rare for a Swedish family to invite a stranger to drop in and take pot-luck. They are so house-proud, that they need good notice to make everything shipshape before offering their hospitality. So, take heart all you foreign businessmen sitting in your hotel rooms at 9 pm. It's nothing personal, just the Swedish way!

Private

When my foreign friends visit me, I invariably relive my first impressions of Sweden and the Swedes of 30 years ago, through their eyes. An outstandingly beautiful country of lakes and forests, with vast expanses of wide open spaces and ample room to breathe in the pure, fresh air. An indescribable light reminiscent of a perfectly exposed photograph. A friendly people on the surface and yet … something is missing. Difficult to say what. No life in the streets, no laughter, few cafés or pubs where you can meet your friends casually over a drink without being ruined. Perhaps they get together in their homes? The dark unseeing windows of the apartment houses stare emptily down on us with blind eyes. Where do people go? What do they do? Do they go to bed at 10 pm? It is all so different, so foreign, to us who come from other parts of the world.

Then there was the interminable waiting. Waiting to be served in the shops, in the restaurants and waiting for the bill. Not to mention the hospitals! Are these the effects of a classless society, I wondered? Those in service had an incredible knack of simply not noticing my existence, or of being much too busy chatting with one another to care. I thought I should never get used to it. 'You will' other foreigners assured me, and they were right. Today I barely notice it until some foreigner comes to town!

Great Britain has for years been one of Sweden's principal trading partners. 'We are so alike and there is no problem with the language', is the explanation often given. But are we? I pride myself on being pretty cosmopolitan having lived abroad most of my life, but nonetheless experienced many of the symptoms of culture shock during the first year. My heart goes out to the thousands of immigrants who come from such vastly different cultures. From cultures where warm personal relationships mean so much more and where people are judged more on their loyalty to family and friends than on their professional achievements.

Making Contacts

I came to Sweden alone, knowing nobody but armed with four addresses of people who had worked with my family. Letters of introduction had been sent in advance but no-one contacted me. After a few weeks I phoned them, one after the other. They were all excessively polite but the conversation ended the same way: 'You must come and see us sometime. Don't hesitate to call if you need anything'. *I needed friends, to be invited into a family, to feel warmth and to have somebody who cared.*

Yes, I experienced moments of black depression and despair, but that is no reason to depress my readers. Most of us have these periods wherever we go when we leave our own countries and frames of reference behind us. We have to acclimatise to other values and attitudes. Instead, let me recall some of my more amusing incidents. An overseas experience can be very rewarding and exciting as long as we remember to pack our sense of humour in our cultural baggage, and are not afraid of making fools of ourselves.

I wanted to fraternise with the locals – to get to know Swedish people. Undaunted by my first failure to make contact, I tried again. My hobby is tennis. I have played on and off since childhood and have always found tennis clubs to be an excellent medium for making new acquaintances. I was delighted to see so many tennis *clubs* listed in the telephone directory and phoned round to see if I could join one. What a disappointment it was when one club after the other informed me that I could hire a court by the hour if there was place, but must find my own partner. But I did not know anyone

'Ssssh! We're playing a match!'

who played tennis! Here was a typical example of how misused the English language can be. They had adopted the English terminology 'club' even 'Lawn Tennis Club' – without giving a damn about the absence of lawns or the social implications of a club. In other words, their clubs were simply public tennis courts.

Finally I found a 'club' which gave me permission to put my name on their notice board: 'Tennis partner required …' I blushed crimson as I pinned it up convinced that others might misinterpret the message to mean even other indoor games! Some months later I was contacted by a woman whose partner had let her down. We should meet on court number 7. If it had not been for people dressed in white scurrying after a little white ball, I should have thought I had entered a mausoleum. The pang, pang of the ball cut the deathly silence like cannon shots. My British sportsmanship was offended when my good shots went unremarked. 'Good shot! Well done! Bad luck!' I cried. 'Sssh! Sssh!' came back at me from nearby courts. They must be playing the World Championships, I thought. However, my charming partner assured me that they were just friendly matches but that everyone took them dead seriously. She never said a truer word. Could I ever adapt to this way of behaviour, I wondered? In my world, tennis had always been an exciting, strenuous game, but above all fun and a healthy way to meet friends, make new acquaintances and relax together.

My new Swedish acquaintance and I relaxed afterwards in the sauna together. As the clothes were peeled off, so the masks began to fall away. Once naked, the women sat close together and engaged in lively discussions of the matches. Unaccustomed as I was to public nakedness, my sense of privacy was sorely put to test! In Britain we strip off in cubicles, or carry on acrobatic feats under bath-towels. If we happen to find ourselves unattired in the company of others, our sense of decency would lead us to pretend we were not there – let alone enter into discussion!

I remember also getting on a tram in Gothenburg and refusing to let myself get off until someone – anyone – had returned my smile.

Their eyes slid away. Why? Were they insulted by me, aggressive to me? I went to the terminus and back. The driver was looking uncomfortable as he shouted, 'Terminus!' for the second time. Finally, a little boy returned my compliment – he stuck his tongue out at me. I surrendered and got off.

Motto for Swedes: Cheer up and start communicating!

Motto for Foreigners: Don't be put off by a sour face
                      They'd love to return your smile – if they
                      dared!

Learning Swedish by Living

When English is your mother-tongue, as in my own case, learning Swedish is no easy task. Most Swedes want to take the opportunity to practise. 'Shut the door! Now I can practise my English!' was an usual request from my colleagues, once they had got used to me. But should someone enter the room, an embarrassed silence and a stiffening of the whole body and facial muscles spoke louder than words: 'I'm not going to make a fool of myself in front of HIM! He probably speaks much better English than I do!' So *individuals* insisted on speaking English with me and understandably did not want to be bothered to listen to my stumbling efforts to speak Swedish, and *groups* normally ignored my presence and continued their conversation in Swedish.

'You don't need to learn Swedish, everyone speaks English!' my friends assured me. Armed with this knowledge, and without one single word of Swedish, off I set to do my shopping.

I chose the easy way out and went to a supermarket where a variety of unfamiliar-looking packages, all neatly labelled and priced, looked down on me. Blessing the American influence I thought 'even an idiot could shop here'.

It was soon to be put to the test. Despite frantic searchings, nowhere could I find, or recognise, either flour or breadcrumbs. I needed both for the 'wienerschnitzel' which I had promised to cook.

Full of confidence in the knowledge that 'everyone speaks English', I hurried over to one of the salesgirls and, clearly and concisely, explained my quandary. Looking like a frightened rabbit, she scurried away into the depths of the store to fetch a handful of colleagues. Pandemonium broke loose. They all stared at me as though I were something the cat had brought in and then proceeded to discuss my problem, gesticulating wildly and pointing to one sad-looking package after another. Finally, a shy nordic-looking beauty eased herself out of the group and came uncertainly towards me.

'I speak a little English', she explained modestly.

'Flour?' I asked and smiled reassuringly at her. A light of recognition shone in her eyes as she pointed out the packet.

'Breadcrumbs'? I continued hopefully. This obviously completely confounded her. But she was not to give in so easily.

'Breadcrumbs?' she screeched shrilly, addressing all the customers in the shop. Everyone stopped shopping and twenty pairs of eyes stared at me while complete shocked silence descended. Suddenly the cry appeared to be 'action stations'. Everyone began talking at once and their helpfulness and kindness overwhelmed me. Nobody knew what breadcrumbs were, but they would jolly well find out even if it killed them, and myself, in the attempt. Most Englishmen and Americans talk louder and louder when they are not understood. Perhaps they hope that the words will eventually force themselves into the foreigner's head. In my case, this is not so. I carry on a kind of mime. People stood transfixed – paralysed, watching my expressive movements.

'Ah' cried a young man 'Yes! Yes!' and proudly presented me with a packet of figs. I dare not think what he guessed I was doing! In desperation I bought a loaf of bread, which I did not need, and

31

began crumbling it. Twenty willing hands then drowned me in breadcrumbs.

I returned home to my friends exhausted but proud. Proud until I dished up the 'wienerschnitzel' coated with the packet of flour, clearly marked 'florsocker' – icing sugar!

Motto: You don't need verbal language to get into two-way communication, so don't stop communicating just because you can't speak a language. Body talk will get you a long way, as it did to me!

After that experience I began to take my Swedish seriously. In those days, foreigners were not allowed to take time off work to study Swedish for 240 hours with full pay, as they are today. But, aided by the generosity of my employers who presented me with a 50 year-old Swedish Linguaphone Course and a book entitled 'Practical Swedish', I got down to it.

I shall never forget my Swedish Linguaphone Course which taught me that grandmother was both a 'mormor' and a 'farmor', that grandfather was both a 'morfar' and a 'farfar', that uncle was 'farbror' and 'morbror' and that aunt was 'faster' and 'moster'. I used to practise on the poor chauffeur of the company where I worked. I would sit in the back seat of his car and try it out.

'Herr Olsson, hur mår din mormor?' (Mr. Olsson, how is your mother's mother?).

And poor Herr Olsson! A red blush creeping up the back of his neck brightening up his grey uniform, replied: 'Bra, tack, Fröken Phillips', (Fine, thank you, Miss Phillips.)

The next day I had advanced to:
'Herr Olsson, hur mår din morfar?' (How is your mother's father?).
And he replied sombrely,
'Tyvärr, han är död!' (Unfortunately, he's dead!).

My Swedish Linguaphone Course paid so much attention to teaching foreigners the importance of relationships and titles, that it neglected the emotional necessities of life, and I was therefore unable to say how sorry I was!

My '*Practical* Swedish' taught me, on the other hand, such useful phrases as 'Var är soldaterna? Jag är sårad. Skaffa hjälp!' (Where are the soldiers? I am wounded. Get help!), which I found rather difficult to apply in the everyday language of this peace-loving, neutral nation.

Motto: Learning a language is not just learning words. You must know how, when and where to use them.

I was beginning to understand a little Swedish, but my acquaintances still insisted on speaking English with me. So when one of them invited me to her 'summer house' I anticipated a stately residence with staff, and packed my clothes accordingly. My expectations were based on my previous experiences of summer houses in England and France which only those with very high income brackets could afford. Imagine my consternation when I was confronted with what I could only describe as a 'tool-shed' with one little room, no water or electricity and an even smaller shed, discreetly placed, for the needs of nature.

Some 40% of the Swedes own summer houses, or have access to one, and go back to nature during the summer months, for which they have waited all year. Whether they can afford it or not, many of them choose to be without water and electricity and enjoy the romance of pumping by hand and spending cosy evenings in the light of their paraffin lamps. Their love of nature makes these material things unnecessary.

Motto: Words have different connotations according to our own frames of reference and the unfamilar customs prevailing in other countries.

Dressed for the occasion?

Punctuality

Here I ran into real problems. The very first phrase I learnt was, 'Förlåt att jag kommer sent', (Sorry I'm late), because I invariably was – in Swedish eyes.

Invited with several others out to the country I followed the other cars. Suddenly they all pulled into the side of the road. 'What's wrong' I enquired, 'somebody got a puncture?'

'Oh no' was the reply, 'It's only 6.55 p.m. and we are not invited until 7 p.m.'

Motto: When in Rome do as the Romans do.

Eating Habits

Many surprises await all visitors to foreign countries, until they have learnt to adapt to the customs. I had my share!

My first invitation to a private home was for 8 p.m. I assumed that meant dinner and arrived starving, only to be confronted with coffee and biscuits! The next invitation was for 7 p.m. This time I took my precautions, ate a hefty meal in advance only to be served a 3-course dinner!

Crayfish are wonderful, if you know how to eat them. I did not. Once again, I was ravenous and began to attack these hard, sharp-shelled little monsters. But my fingers soon became skinnless so I gave up, assuming that we would soon move on to the main course. Visions of a large, juicy steak consoled me while I listened for hours to the sucking sounds and groans of delight made by my smug colleagues! At regular intervals they appeared to remember my presence by turning their bleary eyes upon me and raising their schnapps glasses to their lips. The reward for my patience finally arrived – a cup of coffee!

Motto for Swedes: Your crayfish are probably as exotic to many foreigners as sheep's eyes are to you. Some cultures don't eat shell fish. So ask first. Many foreign businessmen come to Sweden in August since they have been waiting for Sweden to open after the summer vacation.

Motto for Foreigners: If your are invited to a crayfish party and are hungry, eat first!

It was during this memorable meal that I was also confronted for the first time with a butter knife stuck under my nose with a large hunk of butter hanging precariously from it. What was I meant to do with it? I had my own butter knife. Should I take the dirty one and offer them my clean one? Should I put the butter on my toast, as I would in France, or on my plate as I would in England? But there was much too much butter for one bit of toast. I have discussed this

'Skål!'

polite Swedish custom with several of my foreign friends since then. One told me that the first time it happened to her there was very little butter on the knife. She went through the same internal questioning as I had, but assumed that butter must be rationed!

Motto for Foreigners: Take the knife offered you, butter your toast with it, hand it back. Your own knife remains untouched! Butter knives are, in fact, only laid at more formal occasions. Generally there are a couple in the butter dish which are passed round as described above.

Conclusion

It was my lack of awareness of the Swedish way of life which caused me many of the disappointments and surprises described. I tried to establish contacts in exactly the same way I had done successfully at home and in other countries. I anticipated that on announcing my arrival I would promptly be invited to people's homes, that they would return my smile, welcome me to their clubs and introduce me into their social networks. What is more, I was totally unprepared mentally to being ostracised by the language. Although my home, England, is only across the water, the importance attached to punctuality and the unusual eating habits were only two examples of the vast differences in cultural behaviour. It is hoped by recording these experiences that foreigners will prepare themselves better than I did for their visit to Sweden. It is also hoped that the Swedes will show more understanding to foreign visitors and open their homes and their hearts to them.

Looking Back

Looking back over 30 years, it is quite incredible how little has changed! My first impressions are still so vivid because, as I said, I relive them regularly through the eyes of new immigrants.

The most notable change is, perhaps, the fact that today Sweden has become a multilingual society with a number of ethnic minorities. Since the mid 1980's, refugees account for nearly two-thirds of the annual immigration. They have brought with them their life styles and eating habits. They have opened cafés, bars and restaurants to suit most tastes and there has been a mushrooming of outdoor places to eat. Neither do they have any hang-ups, like us Westerners, to close early. Yet due to climate and the cost of living which keeps people in their homes, Sweden will still, comparatively speaking, appear dead to those who come from warmer spheres.

Another change is the subjects which are no longer taboo. Amongst others, Sweden's isolationist policy regarding EC, and its sacred cow – neutrality. When I arrived here in the 60's, my natural curiosity to try to understand the why's and wherefore's, was given the cold shoulder. Today, it is questioned and debated at the breakfast table in the kitchen, as it is in the boardrooms and on the streets.

Yet another difference which has changed the family life-style is the fact that more and more women go out to work. They can no longer take those lovely, long holidays on their deserted islands, leaving their husbands to cope for themselves in town.

I didn't realise how Swedish I had become until the other day. I had been sitting in my car patiently waiting for a couple to leave me their parking space. They had the motor running and were deep in conversation, apparently ignorant of the fact that I had been waiting ages for them to make a move. My passenger was an Englishman on his first business trip to Sweden.

'Why don't you get out and ask him when he's leaving?' he enquired.

'You don't do that in Sweden', I replied. 'You just wait!'

'Why?', he asked. I was stunned as I had no answer.

Brazing myself, I approached the car, put on my most polite, irresistable smile and gesticulating wildly, mouthed: 'Are you leaving?'. The couple stared at me as if I had descended from Mars. It was a hot summer evening, and since they obviously had no intention of opening the window to reply, I tried again shouting this time and using body talk which would surely have won any charade game. To absolutely no avail. They turned away and continued their conversation, looking slightly embarrased!

My English colleague was astounded. To him it was just incredibly bad manners. To me, something much more elusive and difficult to explain to an outsider – the Swedish way for which, unfortunately, I was quite prepared!

Let me give you another example. A few months ago I was involved in a rather bad motor accident. Damages to the car were devastating, but to me and the family only superficial, so I went to work. My forehead, where I had gone through the windscreen, was full of bumps and cuts. As was my nose. My hip, which was three times its usual size, made it impossible for me to walk without crutches.

My workshop was with a completely new group of people. When I entered the room, I was greeted by 15 pairs of dead fish eyes. No reference was made whatsoever to my predicament. Feeling embarassed myself, I decided the situation needed an explanation as they maybe thought I always looked that way! Still no reaction – silence! Only one event convinced me that they had, in fact, heard and understood my message. One of the participants, very unobtrusively, offered to carry one of my crutches as I struggled upstairs to lunch.

Both these are good examples of the privacy of the Swede. He does not want to get involved, nor does he mean to offend you in any way. When I first came to Sweden, I was upset by many such incidents as I took them personally. Today, I don't and neither should you. But I must admit, I never cease to be amazed!

3 Facts and Myths about Sweden and the Swedes

Let's take a look at some of the facts and myths about Sweden and the Swedes. What makes Sweden so special and Swedes so very Swedish? Or are they? As an American retaliated when I asked him what the average American businessman knew about Sweden, 'What does the average Swede know about Ohio?' It is a problem that is common to many small countries. Most people have some sort of idea about France, Germany, Great Britain or the United States, but many confuse Sweden with Switzerland. One Englishman I met told me how much he loved Sweden and that he always drove through it on his way to Italy!

Nevertheless, mass-media all over the world appear to find Swedishness an interesting topic. According to a survey made in 1989 by the Swedish Foreign Office, the *Swedish model* has been the object of much scrutiny. Reporters from Latin and Central America wondered whether a similar system could help them solve some of their social problems. A Kentucky newspaper wrote 'What Swedish parents get for those tax dollars is eye-popping'. And while Central and Eastern European countries were debating the adoptation of the Swedish model, the Western European media claimed: 'It is cracking at the seams. More Swedes are growing increasingly unhappy about their day-to-day dealings with the Welfare state.'

Much attention was also given to Swedish investments in Europe. The Norwegian press claimed 'The Swedes buy Oslo'. Referring specifically to the heavy investments made by industry in the EC, the German press wrote: 'No other country has acquired companies and properties so aggressively as Sweden.' In company with the Belgian and French media, they called it "The Vikings' second invasion." The British, blaming the phenomenon on the Swedish Government's indecision regarding their EC policy, explained 'Swedish industry is in a mood of uncertainty and apprehension.'

Otherwise, most of the articles covered the hunt for Prime Minister Olof Palme's murderer and the trial against Christer Pettersson; the Bofors weapons' export to India; the visit of Raoul Wallenberg's relatives to Moscow and Sweden's solutions to environmental problems. Comparing the Irish environmental laws with those of Sweden, an Irish reporter fanticised:

> There are probably small decorative graveyards for worn-out Volvos, with gravestones made from radiators, wreathes of inner tubes and inscriptions 'Rust in Peace'!

Several other ironical articles described 'Sweden's sick workforce' that takes more sick-leave than any other in Europe, and the luxury yachting holidays offered to our hardened criminals.

The Financial Times summarised the *Swedish model* like this:

> Too many foreigners write about Sweden as if the country were a young, glamorous blonde who has to be saved from old age through constant flattery. In fact, Sweden is a living, dynamic country that is going through a period of rapid change under the stimulus of external economic forces beyond its control.

Sweden

There are two myths about Sweden:

1 As the paradise of a capitalistic-socialist state where the sweet fruits are there for the rest of us to pick if we but follow the Swedish example.

2 An inverted version of the first depicts Sweden as Paradise Lost, the supreme example of the manifold evils inevitably produced by the Welfare state.

Any scholar who has an extended acquaintance with Sweden knows that both stereotypes are hopelessly distorted, and that one should therefore avoid exaggerating either the accomplishments of the Swedes – which are impressive – or their deficiencies – which are real. In other words, the outside world should restrain the urge either to copy or to curse Sweden. Instead it should try to understand and learn from the Swedish experience if only because Sweden is an interesting example of causes and effects that touch the entire Western world.

One of the main reasons given for this state of affairs is the historical abruptness, rapidity and thoroughness of the modernisation process that took place in Sweden. The transformation of Sweden from one of the poorest countries in Europe to one of the most affluent, a change that has taken place largely in the past 100 years, is a rags-to-riches story.

But Sweden is a paradox. Despite the long period of Social Democratic rule, nearly 90% of industrial output comes from private firms. It is a capitalist nation and has given birth to many well-known multinational corporations, which have helped make it one of the most affluent countries on earth. At the same time, it has the world's strongest trade union movement and has a larger, more influential public sector than virtually any other Western country.

The material standard of living has been raised and the worst of the age-old social insecurities – poverty, starvation, inadequate housing, and unemployment, to mention a few – have been greatly reduced. At the same time, however, the modernisation process has disrupted the *personal* intimacy that characterised traditional family, neighbourhood and individual relationships at their best. These relationships were taken for granted by immigrants in their own countries, and the lack of importance given to them in Sweden causes great suffering and isolation. As one of the 12,000 Assyrians[1] said: 'To come to Sweden is like flying 100 years forward in time … When problems arise, our people depend on each other. In Sweden, however, it is the social insurance system that cares for people'.

There is still unemployment – 2.6% today. The economic outlook is grim and the Federation of Swedish Industries is predicting an industrial crisis by 1992 when unemployment may rise to over 6%. The fight to keep down unemployment has been difficult to combine with low wage rises. High inflation and reduced competitiveness are consequently Sweden's main economic problems of the 1990s.

There is wide-spread use of alcohol accentuated by drug abuse, absenteeism and dissatisfaction in working-life. After a tax reform voted in 1990, most employees will cease to pay national income tax, while marginal tax will be reduced to a maximum of 50%. Municipal taxes remain unchanged. Value-added tax (VAT) on most goods and services is 25%. Employers pay social welfare contributions, totalling about 40% on top payrolls.

But these problems are not peculiar to Sweden. They are in fact characteristic of most advanced industrial societies and taken together they constitute what could be called the backlash of modernisation.[2]

The good boy, or goody-goody, at school is never very popular. One difficulty has been that in many countries Sweden has been over-praised for its solutions to many of modern society's problems. Politicians the world over have dangled 'the Swedish model', in front of the eyes of their opposition. The opposition has then retaliated by using Swedish failures and problems as warning signals. Their mass-media have come over to Sweden intent on pricking the Swedish bubble, rubbing their hands with joy when their photographer could dig up a Swede – preferably unemployed, poor and drunk – who could 'tell the story' behind the affluence.

The knowledge that the State guaranteed their security from cradle to grave compared with other countries, lulled the Swedes into placid acceptance of their exhorbitant taxes. But studies have now shown that many EC countries have systems which assure their citizens cheaper health care and security for vastly lower taxes. Pensions and grants for children are still higher in Sweden, but so is the cost of living. *(See Tables 4.2 and 4.3 page 55)*.

Swedish is an isolated language and Sweden's geographic position on the northern edge of Europe, history, neutrality and non-alignment with the EC and NATO organisations amongst others, does little to help this feeling of isolation. No wonder that so many Swedish managers often complain that they feel like outsiders at international gatherings!

As 1992 approaches, Sweden often appears to have fallen off the world map altogether. A deluge of articles and books refer to the new legislation and strategies adopted by the EC and even by Central and Eastern Europe. But Sweden and the other EFTA countries are not making any news. The fact that the Swedish Government intends to apply for membership and hopes to be accepted by 1995, is received with mixed feelings. Those in favour know the dangers of political and social isolation, of not being in the hum of things, and of not being able to have one's voice heard. Others still naively believe that the 'Swedish model' is best. That our food is of higher quality and is less adulterated than those of the EC countries and that we should continue to restrict imports. That our State Welfare is superior and our environmental laws stricter. They believe that, should we become members, our two centuries of neutrality will be at stake, our women will return to the kitchen sink, our popuation drink itself to death with the cheap, unrestricted sales of alcohol, and that our wonderful coastline will be bought up by boisterous, un-private, pushy people!

But Brussels beware! It is rumoured that the Swedes intend to protect their own people from your unhealthy ways by persuading the Community to adapt to the 'Swedish Model', including their restrictive drinking practices, and even their snuff (wet tobacco).

The Swedes

Now let's study some of the stereotyped notions that foreigners have about the Swedes. We can perhaps knock them on the head once and for all by looking at them from the cross-cultural perspective. Here they are summed up in one short paragraph:

There are about 8 million Swedes all of whom are tall, blond blue-eyed and socialists. They make love (sin) all day long, pausing regularly to imbibe schnapps. They then work efficiently and honestly to earn enormous salaries, which makes them such bores that they kill themselves!

Swedes are all tall, blond and blue-eyed

Everything is relative, since how one person experiences another is determined by the expectations and norms of the perceiver. The average height of a Swedish man is 1.79 meters and a Swedish woman 6–8 cms shorter. This may well be considered tall by some races, such as the Asians whose average height is less than this, but not by others. The Swedish Lapps, or Sami as they like to be called, account for some 17,000 of the population and are generally much smaller.

Until the 60's, the Swedes were ethnically more homogenous than the people of most other European countries. They were descendants of the Germanic tribes that settled in Scandinavia thousands of years ago. From the Middle Ages up to World War II there were only small waves of immigration from Germany, France, Belgium, Scotland and Finland. Today there are over one million foreigners, or second generation foreigners, living in Sweden, so more and more brown eyes are mixing with the blue. As in most of the industrialised countries, many of these foreigners are employed as workers in industry and carry out other menial tasks which Swedes refuse. Many are, in fact, highly qualified people but only a few have management positions. Employers make 'poor knowledge of the

Swedish language' and 'difficulties to compare academic qualifications' their excuse for not promoting them, but is it not more likely to be less of a risk to employ 'the devil you know than the devil you don't?'

'You'll easily recognise him, he looks like a typical Swede', is an all too common phrase used indiscriminately. Just as we Westerners generalise that all Arabs and Asians look alike to us, so do we Westerners look alike to them. It is easy to fall into the trap of one of my clients who was to be met at Seoul airport. This was to be his first meeting with the Koreans and he described himself as he would in Sweden by saying, 'I don't look at all Swedish, but I'm easily recognisable by my baby-face. I'm fairly small, dark and middle-aged.' Whereas he may easily have been recognised in Sweden by Swedes with this description of himself, it is doubtful that the Koreans had any help of it at all! How does a typical Swede look to a Korean? What does a baby-face look like? Is 1.70 meters fairly small to them? How dark is dark? And what is considered middle-aged in Korea? The Swedish expectation of life is one of the highest in the world – 74.2. years for men and 80 for women. In South Korea the statistics given are 66.2 years for men and 72.5 years for women. The Koreans retaliated by telling my client merely to 'walk slowly out of the airport' and they would be able to identify him. This really confused him. How would they manage? He discovered the answer on arrival when millions of passengers, the majority Koreans, bustled about like ants to leave the airport. He was the only one walking slowly.

Socialists

Over 86% of the Swedes voted at the 1988 elections. 48.11% voted for the socialist parties (the Social Democrats 43.2% and Communists 5.9%) whereas 41.8% voted for the non-socialist parties (Conservatives 18.3%, Liberals 12.2%, Centre 11.3% and Green 5.5%). Only occasionally during social democracy's four decades at the helm did the party have a majority of its own in Parliament.

According to the latest polls, the Christian Democrats, who did not reach the 4% required at the last election and therefore lost their representation, are on their way back. Many voters appear fed up with the existing political parties and are looking for new heroes. An ill-matched couple, a Count and a self-made pop record producer and fun-fare Director – confirming the *Swedish model* that men from all ranks of life should have equal chances – hope that the role will be theirs. They are referred to endearingly as 'Upstairs and Downstairs!' Encouraged by the results of two opinion polls which gave them 7% and 11% of the electorate, they call their party the New Democracy. Sarcastic political reporters and colleagues nickname them the 'Discontented Party'. They describe themselves to be the opposite – the 'Contented Party – and some of their campaign slogans are 'lower prices, lower taxes, out with gloom, bureaucracy and traffic wardens, in with well-being and more fun in politics!'

They Make Love (Sin) All Day Long

Thanks to the film producer Ingemar Bergman's films and to the Swedish Tourist Board's brochures showing naked bathing beauties, this myth has lived with us for years. But ask yourself, what is sin? In every country of the world according to their own values, attitudes and religious beliefs, the concept is looked upon differently.

Many countries consider nakedness to be sinful but Swedes feel no shame for their bodies. Bearing in mind that Sweden has a coastline of about 7,550 kms, that there are tens of thousands of lakes, that in the Stockholm archipelago alone there are over 25,000 islands, everyone can find his own private retreat and bathing costumes become superfluous. One Swedish girl told me that she acquired the reputation of being 'sinful' when at university in the United States, simply because she ran around naked after showering with the other girls without covering up as they all did. 'Typically Swedish, she has no shame!' was their way of putting it.

The antiquated English phrase 'to live in sin' originally meant to live together without being married. The phrase still exists but its conno-

'She has no shame!'

tation has changed to mean different things in different parts of the world. Swedes were perhaps first to accept this change. They even concocted a name for it – 'sambo'. They were never more promiscuous than other races, but neither were they hypocrites. They did not hide the fact behind closed doors for the sake of society, nor were they thrown out by their families for dishonouring the family name. On the contrary, they are often too open about it. When presenting their 'sambo' (which means black boy in the English language!) they go into intimate details of their relationship.

In the United States, cinemas advertise 'hard Swedish pornography'. In Sweden the cinemas advertise 'hard American pornography'. The Swedes claim that the Danes are responsible for most of the pornography in Sweden today. In Europe I have seen many a sauna advertising 'Swedish saunas', meaning that they are mixed. In

Sweden I have never seen a mixed public sauna, (although I am told by foreigners that they have discovered a few in recent years). Ask a foreigner to join you for a sauna and if you are aware of his silent signals – the shifty eye – you will notice his embarrassment. Once again your sinful reputation has reared its ugly head and he is convinced it will be mixed.

The 'myth' has become so strong that no self-respecting foreign businessman dare return home and admit that he has not experienced it. 'So you've been to Sweden?' he is asked by his friends and colleagues with a dirty glint in their eyes. 'How was it?' 'Fantastic!' replies the visitor, rubbing his hands meaningfully, since his manhood is obviously at stake! And so the 'myth' continues ...

My own behaviour has even become affected by it! On a recent visit to the States, the sign in the hotel lobby 'Swedish Massage' appealed to me after the long flight. But I had second thoughts as to what the 'Swedish' part might mean and asked the manager to clarify. Blushing slightly, he explained 'Swedes are always so healthy and have such beautiful bodies ...'

That business relations are affected by the myth of Swedish sin, there is no doubt. A service that is often provided in other countries simply *must* be available in Sweden with its reputation. When foreign customers expect and demand a certain type of service, how many companies refuse to comply if it is a means to filling their order book? That company policy does not officially admit it, unless they can find some other way of explaining it to the taxation author-ities, is another delicate matter. But as I said before, it is individuals not companies who have to conduct business today. The average Swede's attitude to women is often so different from that of his foreign customers that he finds himself in very embarrassing situa-tions. For example, is the overseas contract really dependent upon whether or not they 'go native' and select a hostess for the evening from the restaurant's aquarium?

Asked by an important potential customer to be taken to a restaurant with dancing, a Swedish manager selected a good-class dancing restaurant. After a few minutes the customer pointed to a girl and said, 'I want that one. Bring her to me!' In vain the Swede tried to explain the Swedish way of behaviour. But the foreigner insisted on sticking to his methods. To keep the peace, and with the thought of the contract to be signed burning in his pocket, the Swede approached the girl himself and asked her to dance. He was convinced that by explaining the situation to the girl, she would agree to come over and sit at their table, in support of the Swedish export drive. But he misjudged her 'If he wants to dance with me, he must ask me himself', was her reply. On returning to his table, the Swede was confronted with a very angry prospective client: 'I saw her first, I want her and *you* danced with her. Bring her to me!' Once again the Swede met the challenge and asked the girl to dance. This time, he stopped at the table while dancing and introduced the girl to his foreign guest. She was asked to sit down with them and did.

Imbibe Schnapps

Here too, drinking habits are very tied to cultural behaviour. The Swedes drink schnapps, as do the Norwegians, Finns, Icelanders, Russians and Poles. Beer is traditionally drunk by the Danes, British, Irish, Germans, Belgians and Dutch, and wine by the wine-producing countries. Boundary lines between zones are beginning to blur, however, and the French are drinking more and more beer, the Irish more liquor and the Swedes more wine.

Unlike citizens in the wine and beer countries, the Swedes very seldom drink in restaurants, due mainly to the expense and to the restrictions on drinking and driving. Most of their drinking is done at the weekends at home. Very few will take an apéritif and it is so unusual, even in restaurants, that the wine waiter rarely troubles to offer one to those speaking Swedish. I soon learnt that lesson and quickly go over to English, much to the embarrassment of my escort! He is then obliged to take a quick decision – should he join me and risk his reputation as an alcoholic, or be ungentlemanly and let me risk mine as a lone drinker?

A driver with blood alcohol concentration of 0.02% will normally be fined and have his driver's licence suspended for 6 months to 1 year. When the level is over 0.15%, a one month prison term and licence revocation for 12-36 months is incurred. In fact, 25% of the DWI's (Driving While Intoxicated) are turned in by spouses or neighbours! For people who live in countries where few such restrictions exist, where it is traditional to sit out on the pavements and sip one's drink, whose life-style is the daily apéritif and wine or beer with the meal, the Swedes would appear to have no drinking culture. Unused to this type of freedom, they unfortunately overdo it sometimes abroad when trying to act like the natives.

In fact, Sweden's problems with alcohol are very moderate compared with other countries. They are only the 28th nation on the ranking list of alcohol consumption. Although I am warned that these are *official* statistics and do not include moonshining, smuggling or tax-free drinks. For obvious reasons, such statistics are not available – luckily for the 'Swedish model'.

But they do have a problematic relation to alcohol. Teetotallers are over-represented in Parliament. Not so long ago every third M.P. belonged to the temperance movement so everyone had to bow down to them and alcohol has become a politically-inflamed subject in Sweden.

A hush-hush policy exists around the whole subject of drinking, probably due to the government's double standards. On the one hand they forbid all advertising of alcohol in Sweden and the monopolised state-owned shops decorate their windows with soft-drinks and posters pointing out the dangers of drinking. On the other, the revenues they earn from it each year amount to 14% of the income and property tax! On every bottle of Swedish-made schnapps the State absorbs 93% of the sales price. On a bottle of whiskey, 90%. Unabashed by their self-enforced restrictions on the Swedish market, they are gleefully rubbing their hands at the success of their gigantic advertising campaign for Absolute Vodka in the United States.

Table 4.1 [3] **Sales of spirits, wine, and beer in litres per inhabitant in some countries. 1987.**

Country	Total litres alcohol 100%	Spirits litres alcohol 100%	Wine litres	Beer litres
1 France	13,0	2,3*	75,1	38,9
2 Spain	12,7	2,3*	54,0*	64,5*
3 Switzerland	11,0	3,0	49,5	69,3
4 Hungary	10,7	4,7	21,5	100,2
5 Belgium	10,7	2,1	23,0	121,1
6 West-Germany	10,6	2,2	25,8	144,2
7 East-Germany	10,5	5,0	10,0	145,0
8 Portugal	10,5	0,8	64,3	40,0
9 Italy	10,0	1,0*	79,0	25,6
10 Austria	9,9	1,4	32,1	118,3
11 Denmark	9,6	1,5	20,6	118,1
12 Bulgaria	8,9	2,8*	22,5*	66,4*
13 Argentina	8,9	1,0*	58,1	18,5*
14 Australia	8,8	1,3	21,0	108,2
15 Czeckoslovakia	8,6	3,3	13,7	130,0
16 New Zeeland	8,3	1,6	15,3	121,7
17 Netherlands	8,3	2,1	14,6	84,3
18 Canada	7,8	2,5	9,8	81,1
19 USA	7,6	2,4	9,0	90,1
20 Romania	7,6	2,0*	28,0*	44,0*
21 Yugoslavia	7,6	2,0*	25,0*	51,0*
22 UK	7,3	1,7	11,0	110,5
23 Poland	7,2	4,7	8,4	30,4
24 Finland	7,1	3,2	5,1	68,1
25 Japan	6,3	2,3	0,8	43,2
26 Cyprus	6,3	2,4	13,2	46,6
27 Uruguay	5,5	1,6	25,7*	20,8
28 Sweden	**5,4**	**2,0**	**11,8**	**51,5**
29 Ireland	5,4	1,7	6,0	75,0*
30 Greece	5,4	–	31,8*	32,3
31 Chile	5,2	–	35,0*	20,7
32 South Africa	4,4	1,0	9,0	46,4
33 Norway	4,4	1,3	5,9	51,4
34 Iceland	4,1	2,4	6,8	16,0
35 Venezuela	3,7	–	0,7	72,4
36 U.S.S.R.	3,2	1,6	5,7	18,2

* Estimated.
,0 The decimal may be unknown.

From 1st January, 1981 alcoholic beverages are no longer tax-deductible under representation allowances. The high cost of alcohol will, it is hoped, dissuade companies from this type of entertainment. To set a good example, official receptions threaten to be even 'drier' than they were!

Willy Breinholst, a Dane, had this explanation of Scandinavian drinking habits:

... Scandinavians are not particularly addicted to drink. Norwegians drink beer and wood alcohol, Danes drink beer and schnapps, Swedes just drink. When a Dane has downed three drinks he starts singing, after six he speaks fluent English. When he has had nine, he doesn't want any more. Should you urge him, however, he will always agree to have just one more. When he has had twelve drinks he will draw you into a corner and tell you in mildly scandalised tones how hard they hit the bottle in Sweden and Norway. When a Norwegian has had twelve shots he will be beyond telling you anything at all, even something about the Swedes. When a Swede has had three drinks he will invite you to dinner, after six he will call you by your first name, enrol you as a member of his family and regard you as his brother. When he has finished his twelfth drink he will cry his heart out because he can't drink another twelve.

An engaging Scandinavian trait is that they will never drink unless there is some special occasion for doing so. Among acceptable occasions may be mentioned: When it is hot; when it is cold; when in a good mood; when feeling ill or in a bad mood; when somebody says you are looking tired and ought to have a pick-me-up; when you feel like it; when it's a long time since you had a drink; when you've just had a drink and want another.[4]

Efficient and Honest

The connotations of both these words are totally different according to your own cultural frames of reference. So if you ask 30 different nationalities their interpretations of *efficiency* and *honesty*, you will probably get 30 different answers.

Swedish businessmen, like many others, consider it *efficient* to hold meetings, prepare agendas in advance, and *honest* to stick to them. Whereas to businessmen from some other parts of the world this behaviour may be considered *inefficient* and *dishonest*. 'Why was the agenda prepared in such detail in advance? – It is inefficient to leave no room for intuitive, creative ideas. Why did they insist on sticking so feverishly to it? They are obviously trying to impose their conditions on us, pull the wool over our eyes, and leave no room for negotiation. It's dishonest. Why hold a meeting at all? We could have worked out these details together, once we had become friends.'

The Swedes have such a reputation for honesty that when the Bofors-India arms business blew up, it made headlines all over the world. Other countries, who committed similar offences but who do not enjoy the same 'Sunday school' reputation as that of the Swedes, received no international press mentions.

Earn Enormous Salaries

Although the Single Market is only two years away, salaries do not yet show any signs of 'levelling out', according to the latest figures produced by Employment Conditions Abroad.[5]

Sweden remains the lowest country in purchasing power terms – firmly anchored at the bottom of the table by a combination of high income tax and a high cost of living. Take a look at the following tables which give the salaries of a senior manager, married with two children, in a company whose turnovover was around 86,5 million dollars in 1990. The survey has only considered one career and has not taken into account any possible career of the spouse.

Table 4.2

Country	$ gross pay	$ net pay	$ buying power
1 Switzerland	119 757	90 130	77 611
2 Germany	97 502	68 015	60 356
3 Belgium	87 810	56 700	50 449
4 Denmark	82 643	39 489	39 923
5 USA	82 462	56 823	56 823
6 Italy	81 658	53 325	47 078
7 France	75 487	57 126	50 536
8 Spain	75 399	52 004	46 119
9 Netherlands	75 349	59 185	53 200
10 Finland	73 128	45 320	38 778
11 Sweden	**67 819**	**34 679**	**29 965**
12 Canada	67 269	44 585	40 134
13 Norway	60 448	42 246	36 406
14 Ireland	59 457	36 291	32 204
15 UK	58 716	43 760	38 815
16 Australia	58 178	37 032	32 967
17 S. Africa	38 170	25 905	31 286

The table below shows how the prices of individual items differ from country to country in 1990.

Table 4.3

Item	Australia $	China $	W.Germany $	Hong Kong $	Netherlands $	**Sweden** **$**	UK $
Pint of milk	0.42	0.68	0.49	1.04	0.38	**0.55**	0.51
Loaf of bread	1.40	1.38	2.08	1.06	1.33	**4.43**	1.02
Bottle of whisky	19.56	31.16	14.27	14.48	16.01	**41.52**	18.53
Tube of toothpaste	2.19	4.00	2.08	1.31	1.88	**2.86**	1.91
Petrol per litre	0.61	0.19	0.87	0.89	1.06	**1.25**	0.91
Meal-dinner for one with glass of wine	29.05	25.00	30.55	25.47	33.79	**53.59**	36.80

Bores

Making 'small-talk' is hardly the Swede's 'cup of tea'. How could it be in a country where the Swedish word for it is 'cold talk' or 'dead talk'! Language affects the way we think. The way we think affects our value systems which, in turn, influences our behaviour and results in the comparatively silent Swede.

Many prefer to keep quiet if they find nothing worth saying, and suffer in silence while others compete for the floor. They have often been compared with the tomato ketchup bottle – particularly after a couple of drinks. You shake and shake and nothing happens, then SPLOSH, it all comes out at once!

The amount of 'small talk' exchanged between people, when, where and if it should be undertaken at all, differs from individual to individual and from country to country. As does the type of small talk. A polite topic of conversation in one country, may well be impolite in another.

What is more, the Swedish school system in the past has not encouraged the students to ask questions. They are loathe to intrude on other people's privacy. To the banal question-and-answer game 'How are you?' – 'I'm fine, and you?' the Swede will often cut the game short by merely answering, 'I'm fine.' He's a practical, down-to-earth creature and knows well that nobody really cares how he feels anyway!

He has also been taught neither to criticise nor contradict others in public. Whereas an Englishman might well attack a proposal made with 'Bloody nonsense!' the Swede would be inclined to take it personally. In other more expansive cultures this rather passive, silent approach could well be misinterpreted as being boring, arrogant or even downright dishonest. When a Swedish Ambassador shouted 'Nonsense!' in a court hearing, and one of the Ministers replied 'Watch it!', the Swedish media had a field day and made it front page news.

If you ask a Swede if he has had a good vacation, you will often get the reply: 'Fine! Peace and quiet!' Sounds boring to many, but what could be more relaxing than a long stroll in the woods, or sitting on a cliff, looking out to sea and philosophising on your isolated island?

Kill Themselves

The Swedes are probably world specialists at statistics.[6] Many countries whose religious beliefs lead them to believe that it is a sin or a crime to take one's life, keep no official statistics of suicides. Of those who do, Sweden was ranked as eleventh on the list.

Table 4.4

Hungary	45.3	per 100,000 inhabitants
Austria	28.3	
Denmark	27.7	
Finland	26.6	
Belgium	23.8	
Switzerland	22.8	
France	22.7	
Japan	21.1	
W.Germany	19.0	
Czechoslovakia	18.9	
Sweden	**18.5**	
Norway	13.9	
USA	12.3	

The other EC countries were ranked as follows:

Netherlands 11.0, Portugal 9.2, UK 8.9, Ireland 7.8, Italy 7.6, Spain 4.9 and Greece 4.9. I found no statistics for Luxembourg.

In fact, according to the Book of World Rankings, Swedes are the most happy people in the world. 33% are extremely happy and 32%

are content with their standard of living. This is twice as many as the average for the European Community countries where the least contented are the French with only 7% very satisfied and as much as 47% discontented opposed to the Swedes' 15%. Only 1% of all Swedes think their lives are very miserable, which is the lowest rate in Europe.

Let's look at a few more fascinating statistics while we are at it. Swedes are top of the list when it comes to drinking coffee and juice, eating frozen foods and buying newspapers. Second in consuming paper products and third in reading books and owning telephones. However, Swedish women rank bottom of the European list when it comes to large breasts! Only 2% of them take D-cup bra's (giant size), whereas 25% take an A-cup (small size).[7]

4 Swedes As Others See Them

Warning! Before reading these pages and finding their content unduly negative, let me stress yet again that the purpose of my interviews was to discover the most common *problems* faced by foreign businessmen in their encounters with Swedes. I needed to document the problems in order to analyse them, relate them where possible to cultural differences in business and social behaviour, and create awareness of them. The material was to be used as a basis for my training programmes.

I am fully aware, and so should you be, that most people find it all too easy to pinpoint problems and criticise others – especially when the others are not there. Due to this I have only taken up experiences which are *recurrent* ones. If you ask for problems, the respondent will invariably give you those communication patterns which differ most from his own. So by learning how he interprets – or misinterprets – your particular communication style, he holds up a mirror for you to see his!

The fact that I was a foreigner asking about the Swedes and knowing them well made it easier – respondents didn't have to mince their words or be diplomatic. Following my initiative, many Swedish university researchers and scholars have since carried out similar studies. In fact, I get about 50 enquiries every year from those carrying out such studies, asking for guidance! I sometimes wonder if my name is posted up on university boards, or am I maybe the only person who is willing to take the time? Although most of them come to much the same conclusions, the fact that they are themselves Swedes, makes it difficult for them to step outside their own culture to do the analysis. We are all blind to our own culture which is what makes objective research so problematic. Ideally, researchers should have lived and worked in the countries concerned to know them well, but not be a citizen of them!

The interviews were held on a person-to-person basis. An open interview technique was used, with no standard questionnaire forms and participants were promised anonymity to encourage them to talk off-the-cuff. 171 participants from different countries were interviewed and included agents, buyers and suppliers, locally-employed managers of Swedish subsidiaries, head-hunters, banks and government officials. In England and France the Swedish Trade Offices made appointments for me, but these were always supplemented with my own contacts. Interviews with other nationalities were mainly conducted in Sweden with foreign businessmen visiting the country.

Summary of Interviews with 171 Foreign Businessmen

The 'international' Swedish businessman, who has probably received part of his education at one of the Business Management Schools abroad and has an overseas posting, is usually highly respected throughout the world. He is considered honest, reliable, efficient and, on the whole, good to work with and for.

But this is by no means the case of Mr. Svensson paying short visits to buyers and suppliers overseas. These 'assets' associated with the 'international' Swede are often sources of irritation and misinterpretation. As stated on the following pages, he has the reputation of being:

Inflexible in his negotiations and behaviour – unwilling to discuss and adjust, slow to take decisions, over-cautious, avoids conflict and a stickler for punctuality. Difficult to get to know, hard to work with and for, stiff, no fun, dull and conceited.

Inflexible was the term given to the Swede by practically all those interviewed. Even after I had concluded my report, I found myself sitting next to a New Zealander on the plane. 'Lovely country Sweden', he told me 'but the Swedes are totally inflexible. I make two trips round the world every year, both buying and selling. I place big orders in Sweden but they always make me feel unwelcome as my schedule lands me here in July. It's July or no orders from Sweden as far as I'm concerned. They can't expect me to alter my whole schedule for them, but they do! I have never experienced this fanaticism about holiday periods anywhere else. Even the hotels are totally inflexible. If I come to the dining-room for breakfast at 9.35 they tell me they stopped serving breakfasts at 9.30 in July as most of the staff are on holiday!'

Ms. Svensson, however, does not collect these inflexible labels. On the contrary, she is described – often with a tone of surprise according to the frequency and general acceptance of women in international jobs in the respective countries – as being clever, extremely easy to get on with, modest and fun. Admittedly, comparatively few of those interviewed had experience of dealing with women since there are so few employed in international management. Those that had, often compared them with their masculine colleagues by saying, 'Swedish women are warm, but the men are cold'. Although this was said with a grin, it was usually intended as a compliment to their charm and had no 'deeper' meanings. They went on to explain that they often opened their hearts and their homes to them.

Let's study some of the other remarks made:

Adapting Products

Agents and locally employed managers of the Swedish subsidiaries complained bitterly about the resistance to accepting local advice as regards the need for further investments, adaption of products to suit the market, local conditions of employment etc. Once again inflexibility to adapt their business and social behaviour to meet local conditions.

A French Managing Director told his Swedish head office that pastel shades were needed to sell his product in France.

'Impractical! Attracts the dirt!', was the reply he received.

Maybe a good sales argument in Sweden where cleanliness and practicality are given top priority. But in France, aestheticism is given more importance.

'Take it, or leave it!'

A Japanese agent asked his Swedish supplier to make the product a bit shorter. The reply:

'We'll consider that once we've started making money in Japan! We are the only company manufacturing this product, so you'll have to buy it from us and accept its dimensions!'

When they do eventually condescend to make minor alterations, they are unable to meet the delivery deadlines scheduled for the special order. '12 weeks is our normal time for delivery. We can't expect our factory to produce them any quicker!'

Negotiating

He is totally inflexible in negotiations. He doesn't negotiate at all. He says 'let's discuss my proposal', but has no intention of discussing anything, his mind is made up. He quotes fixed prices and refuses to take into account the size of the order. A large English buyer of lamps stopped buying Swedish lamps due to this, coupled with the fact that Swedish design had stood still whereas the Italians and the Spanish were much more flexible.

This was a common complaint, especially with the Latin and the Arab nations. They implied that the act of bargaining appeared to embarrass the Swede, yet he derived great pleasure himself in squeezing another drop in his own favour. He is keen on knowing all the facts and financial benefits, is practical, down-to-earth and avoids any show of emotion or criticism.

The former Socialist countries, Asians, Africans, Arabs and Latin Americans all complained about the Swede's impatience to get contracts signed. He rarely allowed the time it takes to build up the personal relationships essential for doing business in these cultures. The Japanese added: 'They often insist on detailed written contracts at a very early stage in the negotiations, leaving no room to accommodate unforeseen circumstances and then they do not honour the contract.'

'I'll miss my plane! Sign now!'

Some British and French agreed: 'Many Swedish companies appear unaware of local conditions prevailing on other markets. When they write contracts they take no account of them and include only those conditions which would exist in Sweden. When the unexpected happens, they refuse to honour the contract, claiming that conditions have changed. This naturally puts the prime contractor in an awkward position. Next time he avoids sub-contracting to the Swedes.

Decision-Making

Many foreigners found the decision-making process in companies confusing. Sometimes the traditional view was maintained whereby only the boss could make the final decision. In others it was decentralised and there was a strong sense of industrial democracy. Many claimed that the Co-Determination Law had many negative effects on their business deals and slowed down proceedings unnecessarily.

The lack of a spirit of adventure, the fear to take risks, over-cautiousness and delay in taking decisions and meeting delivery deadlines were other sources for complaint.

'We must discuss it with the Workers, the Unions, the Management ...

A French bank director had been waiting two years for a decision on investments from a Swedish company, despite the fact that all credits had been arranged. During the past six months they had promised a decision every two weeks.

A Swedish group of manufacturers participated in a trade fair in France and large orders were placed. Six months later not one order had been met and the agent stated, 'I shall probably have to cancel half the orders'.

'I wrote a letter asking a Swedish company to give me an offer within 10 days. I sent several telexes to no avail. Finally, I received a letter written in English. They did not get my order,' said a German.

Many examples were given from Germany of successful test marketing. The industries concerned took too long in deciding to produce the quantities demanded and so lost the market.

Personal Relations

An English shipbroker had bent himself double trying to acquire a ship requested by a Swedish shipping company. He finally managed to acquire one, made an offer and set the deadline. He heard nothing from the Swedes until 5 days after the deadline expired, then he received a curt telex, 'No contract.' His comment was, 'Bloody arrogant these Swedes. After all the trouble I went to for them and they haven't even got the decency to write me an explanation, let alone thank me for my pains. I'll damn well not stick my neck out for them again.'

One of the most constant complaints from different parts of the world was that Swedes rarely reply to letters. Even to those requesting information as to whether their range includes specific products. If it did, they sometimes replied, but only after a considerable lapse of time. If it did not, they never troubled to reply to the enquiry.

'Why don't Swedes reply to letters and why don't they keep in touch?' was a constant cry.

Agents and employees of Swedish subsidiaries felt that they were not given enough support and encouragement from the parent company and were left to fend for themselves. They were rarely complimented on their successes, neither were they directly criticised for their shortcomings. They often learned about the latter indirectly when correctional measures were implemented. When the parent company staff visited their subsidiary, too short notice was invariably given. This, coupled with the fact that the stay was always brief, meant that problems were rarely solved, if indeed voiced. The lack of quick and continuous contacts from the Swedish side was stressed time and time again.

'Strange bods, the Swedes', claimed an Englishman. 'Been dealing with them for years but they never keep in touch once a sale has been made. They never phone to see if I'm satisfied, need more, or simply pass the time of day when in town'.

'We Spaniards appreciate spontaneity and someone who is 'simpático' – the personal approach is all important. Swedes are funny in this way. Either they're stiff and terribly formal and you can't get a word out of them, or they rush around like elephants treating us as uneducated peasants and with loud voices acclaim that Sweden knows best.

They are very unpsychological in their approach to us Spaniards. They should try to be a little more open and much more sensitive to other's feelings.

At the start of the reception they hold themselves uncomfortably in a corner with a 'don't approach me' expression on their faces. As the

'I want to go home!'

reception goes on they may well talk with other Swedes in Swedish, but never, never mix. They begin to drink more and more, become loud-spoken and arrogant, use the familiar 'du' form of address and end up helping themselves to the whisky. This, sometimes in company with their wives'!

'The Swedes – well, they're like their products – reliable, good-looking, but hardly any fun. They have a kind of 'Swedish standard' stamped on them', claimed a German.

Latin Americans, Africans, Arabs and certain Europeans complain that Swedish companies often send out too young men to negotiate since it is their belief that wisdom comes with age. The 'young' men concerned are accused of showing no respect for their elders, of being unaware of the hierarchal system prevailing and of acting in an aggressive, dominating manner. The Swedish government or the company involved is then held responsible for deliberately insulting them by sending someone who, in their eyes, is too inexperienced in life to take important decisions. Many a contract has been lost through ignorance of this important fact.

Timing

From every corner of the globe (excluding Germany!) people had complaints about the inflexibility of the Swedish time system. The obsession attached to being on time was considered ridiculous and petty. It pervaded every aspect of the Swedish business and social life.

Despite being advised that most French offices open between 8.30 and 9 a.m. a Swedish director insisted on calling a board meeting at 8.30 a.m.

The French managing director of a Swedish subsidiary nearly got the sack for being consistently 10 minutes late for board meetings. Every time the Swede from head office wasted even more precious minutes by scolding him. 'Let's get on and discuss more important points on the agenda', was the Frenchman's reaction. 'This phobia they have about keeping time reflects negatively on their efficiency. We finish the job on hand, or the telephone call, and consequently arrive a few minutes late, but so what? The Swede leaves the job undone in order to be on time'.

An American: 'I can go along with their punctuality at meetings, but when they take their office habits into my home, confusion sets in. My wife may well be in the tub and I'm still shaving'.

Sticking rigidly to the timetable and to the agenda at meetings was yet another source of irritation. Depending on the nationality involved, this was interpreted as inefficiency, lack of flexibility and even underhandedness. Inefficient because even if it is 5 p.m., a longer sitting would surely iron out many problems. Lack of flexibility – if someone takes the initiative to present a new idea which could well have a bearing on the subject to be discussed, why disregard it purely because it was not included in the agenda. Underhandedness – why finish now and continue tomorrow before coming to an agreement? They obviously want to talk behind our backs!

The Arabs, Africans and Latin Americans all agreed that the Swedes never spent enough time in their countries to do business. They booked appointments too far ahead, rarely confirmed them and never made allowances in their schedules for the fact that some other matters might meanwhile have taken priority, so postponing appointments. The Poles, amongst others, complained that Swedes were always in a hurry to return home, especially on a Friday, instead of staying the weekend to complete the business. The Japanese found it difficult to deal with the Swedes who were always stressed and pushed for time, as it created an disharmonius atmosphere for doing business.

'I get mad when I spend Kr.12,000 on one of my employees and he refuses to stay the extra day because he has promised the family to be home for the weekend', said an American managing director of a Swedish subsidiary.

'Late again!'

Difficulties to reach people during 'office hours' was also a serious cause of frustration. Flexible working hours are not appreciated by foreign customers and suppliers. It was bad enough before, but now it is even worse. 'May I speak to Mr. Svensson?' (8.45 a.m.). The telephone rings and rings while the customer hangs on the line. Sometimes the customer is lucky and the telephonist replies, 'There's no answer, but Mr. Svensson has flexible working hours. He'll probably be in by 9 a.m.' Otherwise he is simply cut off. The same dialogue is repeated at 3.30 p.m. There is no point in phoning after 4 p.m. and on a Friday 2 p.m. is already too late. Not to mention the summer months – July is dead for business, and from end June to the end of August you can't expect replies to letters or even to faxes.

Many European subsidiaries and importers described the chaos that reigned in their office when Sweden shut down for the summer. Not just did they have to cope with angry customers but they had to suffer the traditional gleeful fax received from head office: 'Now we're closing for the summer. A happy summer to you!' Then dead silence for many weeks, so allowing their competitors to take over the market they had built up, and leaving bills unpaid.

Use of Language

In English-speaking countries the Swede is complimented on his English. In others he is accused of not learning the local languages (German, French and Spanish-speaking countries), trying to make do with English and even using it in his brochures. His written English leaves much to be desired.

In France more importance is attached to the inability to adapt to the French mentality, than the inability to speak French. Just as Swedes have earned their reputation, the French have a hard time to live down theirs of being bad at languages. But middle and top management today rarely object to speaking English – especially with a foreigner whose mother tongue is not English. In fact, many prefer foreigners to speak English rather than adulterate their beautiful language! The Frenchman is proud of his language and his culture and enjoys being able to dominate verbally. It depends on which level you are dealing, was the general concensus. If you have to meet factory personnel or technicians, then French is essential, as it is in all written material. Written French was described as 'une catastrophe'! Even some translated by Swedish translation bureaux, as it was a word-for-word translation and not adapted to the French market.

'It is very difficult to make conversation with a Swede', claimed a Frenchman. 'I don't know whether it is timidity or merely lack of general knowledge. In France you can ask even a taxi-driver his opinion and he will always give it and be quite unconcerned whether he is right or wrong. He just says what he thinks. A Swede appears to have so many complexes that he has to analyse his answer first and explain his motivation. There is absolutely no spontaneity.'

This type of remark was pretty universal. Outside his own technical field, the Swede was a bad conversationalist. Whereas the Latins and many like them enjoy a hot discussion and being able to criticise, the Swedes dampened any discussion either by agreeing politely with everything said and never taking initiative to produce their own opinions, or remaining silent.

During a dinner, he would invariably sit tongue-tied, looking uncomfortable, or insist on talking about the job in hand! As the evening wore on his Dutch courage would loosen his tongue and he would start behaving like a bull in a china shop! Telling dirty jokes etc.

Then there is the conceited, nationalistic-sounding Swede. 'In Sweden we do it this way! Swedish quality! Swedish standard! Swedish neutrality! Swedish welfare! Our Swedish products are best – you can rely on them!' These are all too common phrases which infuriate many nations and make them feel inferior.

'Have you heard this one?'

Frenchmen, Italians, Spaniards, Poles, Czechoslovakians, Belgians, Arabs, Africans and Japanese have all complained that they are treated like under-developed countries. Before producing products in France, sly remarks are made about the reliability of the French workman to produce *quality* products. In Spain, ironic remarks are made about *mañana* when writing delivery deadlines into the contract. 'Can you really eat *that*?' and 'I never drink the water in *your* country', are yet other examples where insensitive use of the language earns a reputation of superiority and conceit.

The unpatriotic-sounding Swede was also depicted. 'Sweden is terribly expensive. No wonder comparatively few tourists find their way here. Our taxes are highest in the world so instead of being productive most of us spend our time trying to find the loopholes to avoid paying them. The social welfare system has crippled us. The Swedish model has collapsed. We are in debt up to our eyes'.

Yet another impression was that the Swede was lazy. He often speaks much better English than the average foreigner, but makes no effort to speak it with feeling. He speaks more slowly, weighing his words for fear of making a mistake. 'Those slow reactions drive me crazy', was the constant cry.

In contradiction to his stiffness and formality, the Swede was also accused of being too familiar – of dropping titles. Examples were given from Germany, amongst others, where German managing directors had accepted the 'du'-form when dining alone with their Swedish colleagues in the evening, but the Swedes then insulted them by continuing to use it the next day in the office in front of colleagues and secretaries.

A Frenchman who had done business for many years with the Swedes had this to say: 'There is a kind of shyness in a way, an aggressiveness in others, a kind of superiority complex in some cases, and inferiority complex in others. It seems that you are talking with someone who understands the words but not the meaning'.

Appearance and General Impressions

Many expressed amazement at the sloppy manner in which some Swedes dressed. Germans, Japanese, French, Spaniards and Dutch in particular. A Japanese exclaimed, 'It really surprised me after the conservative reputation they have. But I don't like it. What are they trying to prove?'

Australia
'First impressions – shy, silent and formal – they even wear ties at a barbecue! After a few beers, less shy, less silent and less formal'.

Clothes talk!

France

A Frenchman who had recently become the agent for a Swedish manufacturer of consumer products had this to say:

'I met him at the airport. One would have said a real Viking as he was dressed in clogs, velvet trousers and a bright coloured shirt that didn't match the trousers in any way. I was shocked! In Sweden I didn't react particularly. But since no Frenchman would take a man dressed this way seriously, I had to cancel most of the meetings I had planned with big customers'.

Japan

'There are two peacocks to see you', said a Japanese receptionist on the intercom to his boss. He was describing a couple of Swedes dressed in light-coloured summer suits with bright-coloured shirts and no ties. He had no idea that the Swedish interpreter accompanying them spoke Japanese!

The Japanese dress very correctly and nearly always wear a dark suit with tie. Shirts may be coloured these days.

But it is, of course, not only the Swedes who bend the rules of social convention. The British do it too. A Swedish company sent out a circular letter to their foreign subsidiaries who were invited to attend a week's course. They were advised to come in 'leisure clothes', since a surprise was planned to take them all cross-country skiing and to a fitness centre. All complied, except the British who came in dark suits. When we discussed the subject of clothing, the British themselves remarked on this and said 'you must think we look bloody stupid?' Silence! After some deafening minutes, there was an embarrassed 'Nja..' from the Swedes. This was interpreted for them by me as meaning – 'yes you do!'

Everyone was unanimous that the Swede is very hard to get to know. He is quiet, has an aversion to conflicts, is bound by prestige and scared stiff of making a fool of himself. He rarely admits to being at fault, never apologises and invariably tries to put the blame on someone else. At conferences he is tongue-tied and rarely takes initiative.

Customers and suppliers complained that, due to this, they never knew if he was interested in their proposals, or not. Several examples were given of misinterpretation of these signals, or lack of them, when the business was placed elsewhere.

Rules and Regulations

Swedish bureaucracy, although made light of by some, was stifling to others. It was accused of having minimised the pleasures of risk-taking. It left no room for individualism, original ideas or fantasy. There was blind acceptance of the most petty rules and regulations and no incentive to work due to high taxation and exaggerated social benefits. Why work harder when you don't get paid for it? Why spend your evenings entertaining clients at home when you are neither recompensed nor allowed to deduct the bill from your taxes?

Several Swedish employees working for multinational organisations in London claimed that the main difference between working in England was that there it paid to be an individual. In England everyone was a bit of an actor, unafraid to produce original ideas, use fantasy, or even to be the only one to disagree strongly during a conference. Whereas in Sweden everyone toe-d the line, glancing furtively over their shoulders for other's reactions. Join the flock, the association, the group and put forward *joint* ideas, but never, never stick your neck out!

Sweden's various social welfare benefits appear to be the source of considerable irritation – flexible office hours, holiday seasons, parents' leave, job rotation, right to study, sick leave for yourself or your children, military service, home guard, trade union work – there are now 19 different excuses to take leave.

'It took me a long time to get on well with Svensson. He had always serviced our machines. Then he was given one year of absence to study. Then came Larsson who took paternal leave and we had to start all over again. Last time it was Pettersson … We like dealing

19 excuses for taking leave.

with the same person who gets to know us and our way of working'. When customers complained about lack of service, the Security of Employment Act was often given as an excuse for keeping an incompetent person on the job.

Many took up the surplus of petty rules and regulations. They hit the foreigner as soon as he drives out from Arlanda airport. 'Somebody dead?' asked an American. 'Why?' I wondered. 'All the cars have their lights on. In the States that means they are in a funeral procession'. I heard myself explaining in typically Swedish tones the safety element behind the law. I obviously was not convincing enough: 'I've heard about all your petty laws, but that's crazy!'

A Frenchman added: 'No wonder they take so long to make decisions. What can you expect from a people who allow their Government to look after them from cradle to grave. They are not given any responsibility to make their own decisions. Look at the latest law that parents are not allowed to smack their children and that children may divorce their parents. Because they can't drink freely, they soak themselves when they finally get hold of a bottle. It adds up to the fact that the Swedish Government punishes all citizens for the faults of a few. Our Government involves itself in business, yes, but would never dare infringe upon the private lives of its citizens. There'd be a revolution!'

He went on to complain about the 'red man' at pedestrian crossings. A policeman stopped him crossing at 11 p.m. in Kungsgatan when there was no car in sight. He said, 'I am an adult, I am vaccinated, I have done my military service, I can take my own risks.' The policeman replied, 'The law is the law for everyone. We make no exceptions'.

Conclusions

All these negative impressions make it hard for the headhunters to find suitable local men to place at the top of Swedish subsidiaries. Their reputation of inflexibility makes it none too attractive a proposition. Besides, they are often obliged to work alongside Swedes who have no understanding or interest in the local mentality and conditions.

The interviews depict a country that has drowned itself in the depths of social welfare, turning its inhabitants into standardised robots who, at the push of a button, blindly carry out their duties in slow-motion, oblivious to the obstacles in their path and of the necessity to go round them and recharge their batteries!

It is hardly a flattering picture or spectacular news. Newspapers and magazines have been banning headlines over the years. But when these 'impressions' are confirmed personally by 171 businessmen from Japan, Australia and New Zealand to America, Europe and the Middle East, it is time to stop shrugging shoulders and do something concrete about it.

5 Cultural Differences Which Can Account for Misunderstandings

My interviews have convinced me that many of these negative impressions are caused by misunderstanding and misinterpreting each others' communication signals. 'He *sounds* so bored, *looks* so disinterested, never *shows* enthusiasm' and so on.

People all over the world use their five senses to communicate with one another. They hear, see, feel, taste and smell. But when persons from different cultures meet, they often misunderstand each other simply because they use and interpret these experiences differently, according to the cultures from which they originate.

As human beings they have much in common. They all need to sleep, eat and trade in order to live, but they do it in different ways. They all have feelings, but they show them differently according to their own cultural patterns. Culture *inhibits* or *encourages* different forms of expressions – laughing, crying, showing emotions etc. They all have a sense of humour, but what makes a Swede laugh, in fact, is often totally different from that which tickles an Englishman, Frenchman, Arab or Japanese.

Recruitment personnel usually appoint someone for the job simply on his administrative, technical or linguistic merits. These are considered the essentials for success in his international work. They are totally unaware of the other equally important qualifications needed – flexibility, tolerance for ambiguity, and a respect and curiosity for others' business and social customs.

For instance, a linguistically fluent person who has not taken the trouble to become aware of the meaning given to his gestures, may innocently offend even more than those who do not master the language well. His gestures may well confuse the foreigner by contradicting his verbal message. They may even insult or embarrass him! Although non-verbal signals reflect emotional states and are mainly transmitted unconsciously, they communicate powerfully. Misinterpretation, or the de-coding of them has often been given as the cause for miscommunication. It has been said that they account for some 92% of a cross-cultural communication and that the verbal language is only the background music for them. Many excellent books have been written on the subject.

It would be impossible to cover all aspects of verbal and non-verbal communication, especially as their significance and meaning vary from country to country, but let's study a few of the critical ones: language, intonation, body talk and eye contact, touch and smell, conception of space and timing, appearance.

Language (Semantics)

Single words can have relatively different meanings across cultures depending upon the expectations, values and experience of the other.

If you offer to place a *big* order with a prospective American or Japanese firm with a view to obtaining a rebate for it, how *big* do you mean? What you term *big* is unlikely to be considered *big* by the others. Everything is relative.

If an American or an Arab tells you: 'You can't walk *that far,* take a cab!' How *far* is far? It's probably well within your walking distance.

The Arabic word 'Bukara' means both 'to-day' and 'sometime in the future.'

Take the whole question of 'yes' and 'no'. you are inclined to believe that 'yes' means the affirmative and 'no' the negative. But you must learn not to take these words at their face value as they mean different things in different cultures. In Moslem countries, for instance, 'yes' is often accompanied by the phrase, 'If Allah be willing', and 'no' only means 'no' if repeated at least three times.

In Japan 'no' is practically never used. They will either say 'yes', 'it's very difficult' or use about 20 other different ways to convey the meaning. 'No' to them is a nasty word which may cause the other party to loose face and this is an unforgivable sin.

When a Frenchman says 'Non, c'est impossible', (no, it's impossible), you often take him at his face value. What the Frenchman really means is 'start convincing me', and misinterprets totally the Swede backing down.

A Brazilian Managing Director was very upset when his Swedish counterpart did not keep in touch.

> During the past 7 years, we had met each other or talked on the phone nearly every week. We had, I thought, become close *friends*. I had introduced him to my *family* and all my favorite restaurants where we had fiesta-d. He had introduced me to his family. Now it is 2 months since the project was completed and since then I have not heard one word from him! Last week I heard that he was in Sao Paulo, visiting a competitor and hadn't even called me! Is this a *friend?*

The Swedish Director concerned had this to say for himself when I atttacked him:

> Because he was my *friend*, I didn't want to waste his time when there was no business to discuss. I knew the system we had installed was working, or he would have phoned me. I knew too that he had problems since two of his directors had left and gone over to the competition. If I had phoned him, just because he was my friend, he would have been obliged to leave the office for at least 48 hours to take me home to the *family* and out to fiesta. So I respected his privacy!

Two men from two different value systems. Both appreciating the value of friendship. However, although the word *friend* means much the same thing universally, the obligations that go with friendship differ enormously. One is not right and the other wrong. They are both right – within their own value systems.

The word *family* too is relative. To take someone home to your family in Sweden usually means spouse and one and a half children. In Brazil? The extended family.

Lots more could be said on the subject of language, but that would be a book unto itself. Let me stress one final point. English, as spoken by the English, is a 'please-and-thank you' language. The lack of a word for 'please' in the Swedish language means that you are inclined to exclude it even in English. This omission can well account for your reputation of being curt and giving orders. We have several other useful little words such as '*do* come in', '*won't* you sit down?' etc which will do equally well if you tire of using 'please'.

Two Swedes were sitting in a restaurant, one raised his arm, clicked his fingers, and shouted, 'Coffee!' to the waitress. She took her time to serve them and when she did, banged down the coffe cups on the table saying, 'You must be Swedes!'. Unaware of the not-so-silent signals of anger flashing from the waitress, they cheerfully asked her,

   'How did you guess?'
She replied,
   'You did a filthy sign and didn't say please So, please don't *tell* me, *ask* me.'

Intonation (Paralinguistics)

This includes such factors as tone of voice, stresses, pitch, melody, pace of speech etc. It is not only *what* you say but *when, how* and *where* you say it. Or, in fact, if to say it at all. People are judged by the way they say things. When speaking a foreign language they often unconsciously transmit false impressions. For instance, you may be the most warm, friendly person at heart, but if you *sound* curt, conceited or indifferent, you will be miscommunicating and judged accordingly.

Curt

The telephone is a typical example. It is often the first contact that the foreign company has with you and your tone of voice becomes responsible for your company's 'face'.

How do you answer your phone? Do you shout 'SVENSSON!' down it and petrify the person at the other end? You may think this makes you sound busy and important. But to people who come from other cultures where personal relationships are esteemed more

Do you sound like this?

highly than effectivity, you may merely sound bad-tempered, childish and discourteous.

Many locally employed managers of foreign subsidiaries complained: 'They address us in exactly the same tone of voice as they do our workers! They appear to have no nuances in their use of the English language. They always sound as if they are giving orders, rather than asking for our co-operation.' Here two elements are involved which have caused foreign managers to feel insulted. Firstly, the tone of voice. Secondly, the differences in the hierarchic system – the unwritten laws of who gives orders and who takes them.

Conceited

'In *Sweden* we do it *this* way', (not the ineffective way that you do it).

'*We* have a very high standard of quality control, safety regulations and consumer protection in Sweden'. (Our own products are best. We can't accept all your cheap stuff! We have such a small population that *we* have to take care of our workers.)

'Our standard of living is the highest in Europe, but then so are our taxes! A lot of it goes to help the starving nations of the world. We give them more per capita than any other nation.'

By making others feel inferior it is easy to acquire the reputation of being overbearing and self-satisfied. Once again, it is not only the content of the message, but the tone in which it is delivered that causes the reputation.

Indifferent

Silence can have a whole range of meanings. To the Swedes and those who value it, it is comfortable. It can be used as a sales tactic, as a courtesy to allow the other person time to consider, to reflect

Silence! Are they alive?

and motivate your next move, or simply to search for the right word. But silence talks louder than words and others, who do not consider it a value, often find it threatening and misinterpret it as being aggressive.

'... It isn't only the long drawn out silences, but the blank face and dead-fish eyes that confuse me. I never know if they've heard my proposition, lost interest, are slow-thinkers or just plain indecisive!'

Comments such as these have been received from all over the world. Business has been placed elsewhere on occasions due simply to the misinterpretation that their silence and lack of facial expression meant lack of interest.

The timing of verbal exchanges, the silences which ensue before replying to questions (chronemics), is yet another miscommunication. The Americans use questions to get into two-way communication. Imagine then a conversation between an American and a Swede. I've listened to many and they go something like this:

'What's your name?'
'Göran.'
'Göran? How do you spell that?'
'Er … G … O … with 2 pricks on the O – R A N.'
'You a married man Göran?'
'Yes …'
'Got any kids?'
'Yes …'
'Boys or girls?'
'Both.'
'What ages are they?'

This kind of behaviour flusters the American who is looking for a dialogue, not a monologue. He's longing to be asked some questions so he can show the photographs which he carries in his wallet. The Swede, on the other hand, brought up not to ask such questions, is feeling out of place. Unused to discussing such personal things with business contacts he considers the American's questions to be rather superficial and does little to encourage their continuation.

'Two Swedes could walk down a straight line and never meet. We Americans use questions to get to know each other and find subjects of common interest.'

Body Talk (Kinesics)

This includes such factors as gestures, posture, head movements, gait and facial expressions.

One can go a long way with body talk. I spent two hours on a plane to Paris where I was the only person who was not Japanese. The lady who sat down beside me bowed, introduced herself in Japanese and held out her visiting card for me. 'English?' I asked hopefully. She giggled. From then on, with the help of her Japanese-English-French-German phrase-book, we found out about one another. Everytime she understood something new about me, she stood up and told the rest of the plane about it. With the result that, when nature called me and I had to walk right to the back of the plane, they all stood up, bowed, smiled and applauded!

Facial Expression

According to research undertaken, there is no single facial expression which conveys the same meaning in all societies. All men smile, but the meaning of smiling is different in different countries.[1] The Asiatic smile is not the only one that can signify embarrassment, discomfort or nervousness. Facial expression indicates attitudes to others. The facial expression accompanying the familiar 'Swenglish' phrase, 'You're very welcome', often contradicts the verbal message. The corners of the mouth are turned down, the facial muscles stiffen and the expressionless eyes shift sideways. First impressions are said to be made within 10 seconds and they are hard

Facial expressions should confirm, not contradict, the verbal message.

to eliminate. The guest is made to feel anything but welcome. 'His *face* is like an open book', and 'it was written all over his *face*', should perhaps not always be taken at *face* value. But these sayings are proof of the significance attached to the messages transmitted through facial expressions.

'Ladies and gentlemen, I'm *glad* to *see* so many of you here today.' Yet he looks neither *glad* nor does he *see* anybody since his eyes are fixed firmly on his manuscript! All too often I have experienced this type of behaviour at the opening of international exhibitions and congresses. I cease to listen to the speaker and instead watch the foreign participants' reactions. One thing is certain, the intended message is not getting across, but the myth of being indifferent to the audience and a bore is fast becoming a fact!

Gait

Strange conclusions are reached, based unconsciously on body movement, which can well account for some of the stereotyped notions:

'The Swedes don't work as hard as we do – you never see *them* running in the corridors, banging doors, working till 9.00 p.m.'

'Look at the slow way he moves! What arrogance! How can you stick it? Don't expect me to do business with him, that's all – he'd probably conduct it in slow motion too!' This was said by one importer to another on being introduced to his Swedish supplier.

These examples and others like them, show how people from more temperamental cultures often misinterpret the Swedes' 'slow motion' as arrogance, indifference and even laziness.

Posture

'I'm *open* to recommendations or questions', is a phrase commonly used during international negotiations. But if the speaker is not *open* himself – has his arms crossed, ties his body into a corkscrew and his legs and feet into knots – he will probably be considered inflexible and disinterested in others' viewpoints. Think how some speakers encourage questions while others discourage them. It is often the body talk which influences the audiences, as much as the content and presentation of the speech.

Everyday gestures

Let's look at a few of the more everyday gestures which differ from culture to culture. Do remember though that each gesture is linked to a specific situation and can never be studied as an isolated factor. Its meaning may well differ according to that situation. Awareness of them, however, may help you to understand how easily your own gestures can be misinterpreted.

Nodding. We are inclined to take for granted that such gestures as nodding and shaking the head mean the same to people all over the world. However, in Greece, parts of Turkey, Bulgaria, Yugoslavia, Iran the Arab countries and Bengal, to mention a few, the head toss, similar to our nod, means NO. Whereas the head sway, similar to our shake, means YES.[2]

Greetings. Some shake hands, some do not. Even shakes differ. There is everything from the hand-pump to the limp-fish hand-shake. In Northern Europe people shake hands when they meet for the first time and sometimes when they part. In Southern Europe, the Middle East and Latin America they do it more frequently.

In Australia men shake hands, but rarely with women. In Korea men generally bow slightly to each other and shake hands, either with both hands or with the right. Women do not usually shake hands. In Japan they bow several times and do not shake hands.

In Thailand men and women place the hands together at the chest and bow the head. How high they raise their hands and how low they bend their heads depends on the age and rank of the other person. However, hands are not raised higher than the eyes. A person's head is sacred and should not be touched by others. Although patting a

90

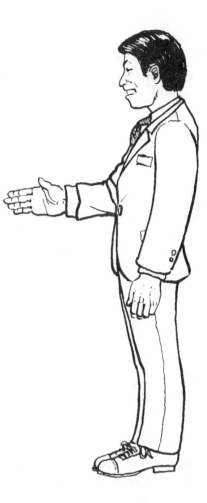

Asian ceremonies are full of pitfalls!

child on the head is a friendly gesture to us, it should be avoided at all costs, nor should objects be passed over someone's head.

In Taiwan and China a nod of the head is considered appropriate when meeting someone for the first time. But for acquaintances and close friends, a handshake is most common.[3]

Indeed Asian ceremonies are full of pitfalls for foreigners but a word of warning would be in place here. Many Asian men and women have been trading with the West for so long that they have adopted

91

the western handshake and in such cases it would be ill-advised not to offer yours. The appropriate strategy is therefore to be flexible and wait to determine whether the Asian is prepared to offer his hand.

Insulting Gestures[4]

As mentioned, certain gestures used innocently by some can be humiliating and insulting to others. The aim of this section is not to map out where in the world such gestures are taboo, but to create awareness of their different connotations. It is hoped by so doing that travellers visiting unknown territories will have their curiosity aroused and be more sensitive to noticing them for themselves.

Use of left hand. In a great many countries of the world the left hand is considered unclean. You will notice that people only eat with their right hands, rolling their food into little balls in the palms of their hands before putting it in their mouths. Their left hands are held discreetly in their laps. Neither do they touch each other, exchange gifts or visiting cards with their left hands. A left-handed Swedish project manager was sent out to the Middle East on a building project. Neither he nor his company were aware of this taboo and failed to understand why he alienated so many of the workers on the project.

Soles of feet. Not as common, but still quite widespread is the belief that the lower you come down the body, the dirtier you are. Consequently in such areas the soles of the feet are the dirtiest and should not be shown. Here you will notice that when sitting on chairs, legs are never crossed over the knees. They may be crossed at the ankles with the feet pointing towards the floor. When sitting on the floor, the feet are discreetly tucked away to avoid pointing them at someone.

Outstretched legs. In other areas it is common for people to sit on the floor, or in the market place, with outstretched legs. To walk over a woman's legs is an insult to her. A Swede told me of the time he unknowingly humiliated an African woman by so doing. The entire market place was in an uproar, angry voices were raised and fists shaken against him.

Wagging and pointing finger. In Northern European cultures, we only wag our fingers at children and feel degraded when people from other cultures wag theirs at us. On the other hand, we often point with our index finger to show the way or draw attention to something, oblivious of the fact that many foreigners find the gesture threatening and even obscene. The statue of Charles XII pointing to the east, which is often photographed and used to promote Sweden indiscriminately throughout the world, causes many a blood pressure to rise!

'Thumbs up'. In most countries the thumbs up sign has come to mean 'all is well' and is frequently used by hitch-hikers wanting a lift. However, in Sardinia and Greece it would not be advisable since the message being transmitted to them is in fact 'get stuffed'. Hitch-hikers in these countries are advised to do as the natives do and adopt the loosely waved, flat hand gesture.

'V'-sign. The same insult is transmitted to inhabitants of the United Kingdom if the V for victory sign made famous by Winston Churchill during the Second World War is made with the palm facing inwards, instead of outwards. Yet most of the rest of Europe have adopted the palm-inwards sign to mean 'victory', with the exception of Sicily, Greece and Turkey where it is more often taken to mean 'two'.

The Circle-sign. An American or Englishman would use this sign to signal that something is OK – he raises his hand and makes a circle with his thumb and forefinger. But in Japan, for instance, it is the gesture for money. In France it means 'zero' or 'worthless'. In Malta it means that someone is a 'pooftah' – a male homosexual – and in Sardinia and Greece it is an obscene comment or insult to either male or female.

Applauding. If, instead of clapping, the applauder taps the back of one thumb-nail against the other, it can be both positive and negative dependent upon where you are. In Panama, for example it is merely a form of silent applause, but in certain Arab and Spanish-speaking countries, it is an act of derision. In England and elsewhere, however, they use the super-slow rhythmic hand-clap to be insulting whereas in Russia, Sweden and other Scandinavian countries it is highly complimentary.

Eye Contact (Oculesics)

Eye contact – length and direction of gaze, both when talking and listening – differ from culture to culture. The Englishman, for example, focuses steadily on the eyes of another person. Whereas the American (more like the Swede) shifts his gaze from eye to eye or away from the face altogether. The Englishman also does much less nodding and grunting than the American. He shows he is listening by his eye blinks and attentive stare.[5]

A Swedish project manager in Saudi Arabia considered the Pakistanis working for him to be insolent. According to him they refused to look him in the eyes when he was talking with them. He went on to reprimand them, unaware that to do so in public would make them lose face. He was obviously unaware that they were in fact showing him a sign of respect. The same Swedish project manager, who was relatively young for the job, insulted unwittingly an older Saudi government official by looking him in the eyes and by using a superior tone of voice. In many of the Third World countries, it is very disrespectful to look your superiors or elders in the eyes.

During an international conference in Stockholm I was placed at the same table as a very beautiful Brazilian woman. She spoke only Portugese and I noticed several of the men preening themselves before making overtures. When they discovered to their horror that they could have no *verbal* contact with her, their eyes slid away and they slithered back into their shells! When asked her impression of Sweden and the Swedes, she replied to the first, 'Sweden is very hygienic' and to the other, 'They have no soul in their eyes'. Her *eyes* compared the hygienic standards in Sweden with those in Brazil. Her impressions of the Swedes were formed purely from the *non-verbal* language being spoken at the table. I am convinced that none of the Swedes present were aware of her uncomfortable situation. They were much more occupied with their own. My advice to those of you who find yourselves in similar positions is to make use of your body talk and *smile!* I can assure you that you can go a long way without words and, more important, make your guests feel you care about them!

Touch (Haptics)

Where, how and how often people touch each other while conversing has been yet another subject for study. Physical contact, in our culture at least, is restricted to young children and lovers. But there are wide cultural variations. Sid Jourard, a Canadian psychologist, sat in coffee bars in four different cities watching pairs of people engaged in conversation. He noted how many times on average they touched each other in an hour. In San Juan (Puerto Rico) 180, Paris 102, Gainsville (Florida) 2 and London 0!

A Spanish exporter told me how uncomfortable he feels in Sweden because he always feels obliged to clasp his hands firmly behind his back for fear of touching someone. Should he slip up, the effects were dramatic – it was as though rigor mortis had set in. The Swede stiffened up from the top of his head to his toes! To Southern Europeans, Arabs, Africans, Iranians and Latin Americans this behaviour is taken as a personal affront. 'We want to show our friendship and esteem, and they snub us!'

A Swedish export manager with the world as his market, admitted that he did not enjoy the best personal relationships in the Middle East. He vividly described his feelings the first time an Arab customer held his hand in the street. 'I felt myself going scarlet in the face. Then I felt the perspiration on my brow dripping down my spine. I bit my teeth together and prayed that the Swedish TV was

'I hope we don't bump into anyone I know!'

not out on the prowl! Nowadays he tells the Arabs that those are not Swedish customs and draws his hand away. 'After all', he added, 'I've taught myself to kiss the hands of my Polish customers' wives, but enough is enough!'

In many cultures it is acceptable to show affection for a member of your own sex by, for example, publicly holding hands. But to do so with a member of the opposite sex is unacceptable. Whereas in other parts of the world the opposite applies.

Smell (Olfaction)

Smells communicate too. You can even smell trouble – if you are sensitive! Certain odours conjure up memories of our youth, such as the smell of baking, and newly-mown lawns, while others are classified as 'foreign smells'. The smell of garlic is often unpleasant to those who come from cultures where it is uncommon to eat it. But those who come from 'garlic countries' probably never notice the smell.

In the industrialised countries we are slowly but surely eliminating all natural odours with sprays. It is not done to 'smell bad' or even to discuss it for that matter, so we install extractor fans and buy sprays and deodorants synthetically perfumed with the fragrance of nature. But to others, these sprays smell bad.

Edward T. Hall, an anthropologist, describes how the Arab may reject the girl he is to marry if she does not smell nice. Not so much on esthetic grounds but because of a residual smell of anger or discontent. He explains:

> 'Arabs consistently breathe on one another when they talk. To smell one's friend is not only nice but desirable, for to deny him your breath is to act ashamed. Americans, on the other hand, (and Swedes) trained as they are not to breathe in people's faces, automatically communicate shame in trying to be polite.'[5]

Space (Proxemics)

People like to keep certain distances between themselves when conversing. Some liken them to porcupines 'they like to be close enough to obtain warmth and comradeship but far enough to avoid pricking one another'.[6]

Swedes, as many Northern Europeans and North Americans, like to keep their distance. If their personal bubble of space is infringed

'HELP! He must be a homosexual!'

upon, they back away or stiffen, so adding yet one more notch to their reputation of being unfriendly and distant. I have seen a Swedish buyer being chased around his desk by an Italian.

International airports and hotel lounges are excellent places for studying different cultures' space bubbles. Not to mention behaviour in lifts.

Notice next time you take a lift how people react to having their space bubble violated. In Sweden, if alone, they will probably place themselves in the middle. If someone enters they will move themselves into the corners and avoid eye contact by firmly fixing their gaze on the indicator. When the lift gets full, people begin fidgeting about uncomfortably to avoid bodily contact.

At times, prestige goes hand-in-hand with space. I remember the controversy that ensued when I was allotted a large office on the top floor of the building, with a fitted carpet and a wonderful view! A privilege normally reserved for top management. Hall explained this situation well:

> 'In *America* top management generally occupy the biggest offices and they are located either at the corners of the buildings or on the upper floors. The *French* supervisor will be found in the middle of his subordinates where he can control them. The top floor of *Japanese* department stores is not reserved for the management – it is the bargain roof!'[8]

An *English* top buyer for a large department store sat in an office resembling a gold-fish bowl, surrounded by packing cases! So, as in the *Arab* world, the location of an office and its size can hardly be an index of the status of its occupant! Yet how easy it is to draw the wrong conclusions ...

Time

Every culture has its own concept of the importance of time. It can be kept or spent, stand still or fly. Some consider punctuality a virtue, while others treat it more casually. When we are late, we have been brought up to apologise for it, and we anticipate that others will do the same. I asked an Iranian if he esteemed punctuality to be important. 'Of course!' was his reply. But I asked the wrong question. What I consider to be 'punctual', may be far from the connotation given to it by an Iranian. When I asked him to specify, he admitted that 'within the hour' was customary. So if he arrives for a meeting within the hour, he understandably sees no reason to apologise. The North European and American attitude is – not just is he very late, but he doesn't even have the courtesy to apologise! And the visitor is baffled to meet an irate customer, who constantly looks at his watch and claims he has another meeting within a few minutes.

This brings us to our next point. The way we plan our time reflects our relationship to it. This applies to office working hours, holidays, religious manifestations, eating habits and so on. In those countries where mealtimes are considered a social occasion and 2–3 hours are devoted to them, business should not be discussed. There is a time and a place for everything, and this is neither the time, nor the place. I remember the illustration a Belgian gave me of how his Swedish supplier moved aside all the glasses, cutlery and plates groaning with food to spread out his prototype plans on the table.

We plan appointments every hour, nearly every minute of the day, months ahead. A fully-booked diary is rather a status symbol for us. We are so present-and-future orientated that we leave no time in our schedules for flexibility. We are so task-orientated and intent on filling our order books, that we leave no time for deepening personal relationships. *Time is money.* Whereas people from many other countries are past-and-present and being-orientated. Destiny controls their lives so why tempt Fate by trying to influence its course? That is why personal issues often take priority over business appointments – especially those booked far ahead. If we cannot accept our destiny, and are not even masters of our own time then we certainly cannot be qualified, in their eyes, to master a negotiation. The company has insulted them by sending out some junior executive to handle their business, and they wish nothing more to do with us. 'When God made time, he made plenty of it.'

Appearance

The old saying 'clothes maketh man' should not be taken lightly. Clothes talk too. They tell us a lot about the person we have in front of us – or rather we think they do. Hair styles, beards, jewellery, decorations and accessories add to the picture that is transmitted. When we get down to business, or want to make the meeting more informal, we often take off our jackets. If the boss joins his staff at a weekend training course, the fact that he is sportily dressed will

Typical!

probably make him more approachable. Once again, our judgements are often culturally-bound. Typical American! Typical Australian! Typical Englishman, we claim, often meaning that they are dressed in the fashion with which we associate that nationality.

Many of us rarely stop to consider how we form our opinions of others and whether we are right. Yet those opinions often affect our whole behaviour towards that person. Both formal and professional judgements can have far-reaching effects. People are selected for jobs, customers choose their suppliers, bankers give credit, social workers decide the fates of their 'clients' – all with complete confidence in their own judgement.

In every instance each article of clothing transmits a signal to an onlooker, telling him something about the wearer's background, mood or personality ... In this way clothing is as much a part of human body-language as gestures, facial expressions and postures.

6 Management Styles

Multinational corporations are facing a comparatively new challenge – how to build up successful working relationships between headquarters and newly-acquired foreign subsidiaries. Between people who often do not even speak the same language, and whose expectations, priorities, ways of doing business and managing people differ too. Both parties can experience communication difficulties and frustrations if they do not share common goals, values and business ethics.

Management styles are a reflection of the culture. Many companies have tried to import the methods practised by the Japanese or by the Americans, with limited success. They can only work if they take into account the national characteristics of the country in which they are applied.

This has been well-documented in research undertaken by the Dutchman Geert Hofsteede[1] and by the Frenchman André Laurant of INSEAD.[2] Their data illustrates the dangers in attempting to transpose the management style of one culture onto that of another. They maintain that parent companies would do far better to attempt to draw the greatest benefits from the unique style of *each* culture, rather than impose their own management styles on their foreign subsidiaries.

Swedish Management Styles

So what is the Swedish management style? Is it exportable and if so, where? All our studies have shown that, comparatively speaking, the Swedish management style is less hierarchical than most others –

103

although this has changed slightly since the soft, flat-style organisation of the '70's. Swedish expatriate managers have discovered that they were obliged to take power upon their shoulders on most other overseas markets — to learn to give orders, make their own decisions and generally throw their weight about. However, Hofstede claims that it is easier to accept power than to give it up. This can help explain the repatriation problems from which many Swedish

Yes Sir!

Listen to us!

managers suffer, and those experienced by foreigners setting up in Sweden.

It is interesting to look at how the Swedish values compare, for instance, with those of the EC countries. Hofstede's research which included fifty countries and three areas, found that managers and employees vary on four primary dimensions.

Power Distance: the extent to which a society accepts the fact that power in institutions and organisations is distributed unequally.

The Northern European countries, including Sweden, are all grouped at the lower end of the scale, indicating their preference for equality. Whereas the Latins – especially France – are much higher, showing a preference for hierarchy.

Individualism-Collectivism: Individualism is characterised by people who are supposed to take care of themselves and of their immediate family only. Collectivism is those who belong to in-groups or collectivities which are supposed to look after them in exchange for loyalty.

Most EC countries are basically individualistic with the exception of Portugal and Greece. Surprisingly enough, Sweden and France score the same on this dimension!

Uncertainty avoidance: the extent to which a society feels threatened by ambiguous situations and tries to avoid them by establishing more formal rules and procedures.

The highest values here are given to Greece, Portugal and Belgium who can be expected to prefer legislation and clearer rules of the game, rather than dialogue. Sweden is at the lower end of the scale, together with Denmark, Ireland and Great Britain.

Masculinity-Femininity: Masculinity characterises the dominant values in society such as success, money and things. Femininity, caring for others and the quality of life.

Sweden is shown as the most femine of all 50 countries studied, with Italy the most masculine of the EC countries. Maybe this 'perfect marriage' of opposite partners explains why Swedish multinationals employ so many Italians to manage their subsidiaries around the world? Sweden's position as the most feministic country is, perhaps, easier to understand if we remember that Hofstede's research represented *overall* cultural values, *not* business culture values.

Recently, Hofstede has added a fifth dimension to take into account the Asian mind. He calls this one Confucian Dynamism.

Now let's look at a couple of examples from André Laurant's work. He asked managers from each country to describe their approach to more than sixty common work situations.

As is seen in Table 6.1, Swedish managers have the least problem in bi-passing the hierarchical line and, certainly do not expect the boss to have *all* the answers. (Table 6.2). They value getting the job done which means going to the person most likely to have the information needed, which may well not be the boss. He cannot be expected to have all the answers. By contrast, most other countries consider by-passing the boss as a sign of insurbordination. To maintain credibility and respect as a boss, they feel obliged to have all the answers to subordinates' questions.

Table 6.1 In order to have efficient work relationships, it is often necessary to bypass the hierarchical line.

Percent disagreement across countries

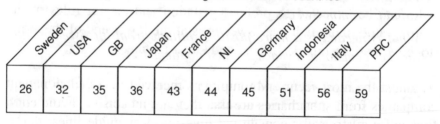

Sweden	USA	GB	Japan	France	NL	Germany	Indonesia	Italy	PRC
26	32	35	36	43	44	45	51	56	59

Table 6.2 It is important for a manager to have at hand precise answers to most of the questions that his subordinates may raise about their work.

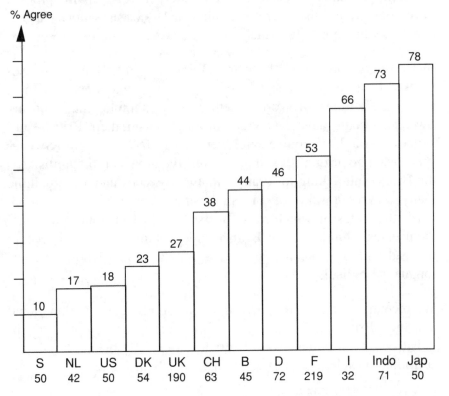

% Agree

S	NL	US	DK	UK	CH	B	D	F	I	Indo	Jap
50	42	50	54	190	63	45	72	219	32	71	50

In another study, foreign subsidiaries of four Swedish multinationals in France, Germany, Great Britain and the USA had this to say:[3]

> It is the Swedish management style that is unusual, not the style of the other countries.
>
> The Swede is a straight-forward person, but impossible to understand for a non-Swede.
>
> What is needed is a more positive attitude from the Swedes, and quicker decisions. Swedes are just not decisive!

Amongst the most recurrent complaints received by Swedish parent companies from subsidiaries are that they are indecisive; avoid conflict; always strive for concensus; give no clear guide lines; don't answer letters and reports; never sack unqualified people; too many decisions taken at too low levels, isolated from the market requirements since sales offices are rarely involved with product development, and that there is an unclear HQ organisation which is constantly being reorganised.

Interestingly enough, we have found that it is often those countries whose life-styles resemble each other most, who experience the most severe difficulties to work together. For example, many of my Swedish clients have had great problems with their British subsidiaries – and, of course, vice versa. The fact that most Swedes speak such good English and have a reserved manner, often misleads the British into taking for granted that the Swedes understand all the many unwritten rules of British business and social convention. Unwritten rules of which most British are, in fact, totally unaware themselves! Similarly, the British understatement is guaranteed to mislead and frustrate the Swedes and even others whose mother-tongue is English!

We recently carried out an investigation for a Swedish multinational and their British subsidiary. It was interesting to attempt to distinguish betweeen which were a) organisational problems, b) parent-subsidiary problems and c) purely Swedish-British ones.

Here are some of our findings:[4]

Swedish-British Comparisons

The Swedish HQ style of participative management means that authority and trust are passed down the organisation. People are given the freedom to make their own decisions. They are team-orientated and loyal to both the company and the team.

The UK subsidiary style of bureaucratic and hierarchical management means that there are detailed job descriptions and written procedures. The multiple levels of management are rigidly observed and there is centralised decision-making. They are individualistic, pursue their own personal career goals and financial rewards.

The consequences of these different management styles are many. For example, if the Swedes are not given the freedom to make their own decisions and meet their own goals, they will ask for a transfer within the organisation. Whereas the British, who have not the same feeling of loyalty to the company, leave if they do not achieve their goals.

The Swedes are seen by the British as weak, indecisive managers, with woolly personnel policies, coddled by the company. (Protection of low performers, personal computors, long vacations.)

The Brits are seen as dogmatic, inflexible, arrogant managers with rigid personnel policies. (Fire the low performer, written permission for petty things like pens and pencils.)

The Swedes are described as accustomed to making suggestions and giving unclear guidelines. Laid back, unemotional, no small-talk and avoid confrontation at all costs.

The British are described as giving orders, centralised decision-making, indirect yet direct, (under-statement) and extremely critical of both HQ and of one another.

The same client also undertook a cultural mapping to highlight different attitudes in their American subsidiary. It is interesting to compare the two and notice some of the similarities on both sides.

The Swedes were viewed as awkward, not comfortable with human relationships, not sensitive to how people feel about work. The Americans were viewed as artists at presenting a good image, combined with concern for promotions and symbols of success. They want to shine like stars! They are felt as unloyal, only out for themselves.[5]

Once again let me repeat, for those of you who skipped over the first pages, that in our interviews we were all asking for *problems* encountered on both sides. When highlighted, they can be analysed and often solved. The interesting conclusion to be made is that both parties experienced these problems, but from opposite angles since they judged from within their own frames of reference.

But the question must be posed. Are these typical parent-subsidiary 'power-game' comments which could equally well have been made, regardless of the nationality of the parent, or are they culture-bound? In fact, Hofstede's research of 116,000 employees from an American multinational, raises questions similar to the ones we present. As does Laurant's. However, we are all unanimous that those managers who are 'culturally literate' have a real edge over their competitors. A good example of this is how the President of a large US corporation defines the differences in the mentalities of the French and the Americans, with the consequent inevitable frustrations! [6]

US-French Comparisons

Obviously there are problems in measuring Frenchmen by the standards of American industry. And vice-versa. As one Frenchman put it, "you Americans are well-trained executives of well-run corporations in the US. But abroad you are not clever enough, not flexible enough, not 'débrouillard' enough (talented, resourceful, literally smart enough not only to pull strings but to disentangle them) to really get along in France. You are not French."

Whereas the American tries to think in a straight line, the Frenchman insists on thinking in a circle. The American mistrusts complex things and tends to over-simplify. The Frenchman, by inclination and education, mistrusts simple things and tends to over-complicate. It is for this reason that no Frenchman, by American standards, can ask a simple, straight-forward question when speaking in public. By French standards, no American speaker can give a full, sophisticated answer. A Frenchman tries to define the question; the American tries to answer it.

A French businessman mistrusts the very things in which an American businessman has the most confidence. Examples? The Frenchman is innately suspicious of the figures on a balance sheet, of the telephone, of his subordinates, of the law, of journalists and of what he reads in the press, of investment banks and, above all else, of what an American tells him in confidence. The American, au contraire, has trust in all these things.

An American executive tends to forget what he's said in a letter. A Frenchman never forgets what he's purposely left out.

An American will probably lose his typical enthusiasm for a project before a Frenchman gets over his typical reservations.

An American businessman treats his company like a wife; a Frenchman treats each of his companies like a mistress. This is particularly true when a firm decides to set up a new subsidiary with a foreign partner. The American wants 100 % exclusivity and control over the long-run. The Frenchman wants 100% flexibility and freedom over the short.

When a Frenchman is polite, he is very, very polite and when he is rude, he is very, very French. But a Frenchman is rude only in public places – waiting for a taxi, in a restaurant, behind the wheel of a car. He is supremely polite in private places – in a letter, at a dinner, when he's being introduced. The typical Frenchman can make a pre-arranged telephone call to a good acquaintance and apologise three times during the conversation for calling. The same Frenchman could dial a wrong number at three in the morning and swear at the person whom he woke up.!

7 Advice to Swedes

In large, the advice I am giving you in this chapter is equally applicable to other nationalities with whom you work. They too need to develop these communication skills, but sometimes in reverse, if they are to function well with you. However, I am convinced that good advice must be based upon the strengths and weaknesses of the individuals concerned and must, therefore, take into account the idiosyncrasies of each person's behaviour.

Adapting yourself

Parallel with the importance of adapting products and marketing strategies to the different markets, is the necessity and ability to adapt yourself in the marketplace. *You* have been selected to help. Many of you admit to being shy, to having a communication complex, to lacking confidence and make these excuses for your passiveness. What astounds me is that so many of you appear to accept your insecurity as an intricate part of your character – a permanent fixture. You happily use it as an excuse to one and all to explain away your communication problem:

'100 years ago we were nearly all peasants scattered over this large country. The nearest neighbour was miles away and our only contact was with family members. We have had so little experience of other cultures.'

But that was 100 years ago! You can't blame your behaviour on your ancestors forever. Start fighting your shyness and build up your self-confidence by finding out more about others. You have been selected for your job because you have the best qualifications for it. Write down all the attributes needed to succeed in your particular market. Then check on how many you possess, build on them and get to work on the others.

If you are responsible for a new market and going there to conduct business for the first time, try to arrive a couple of days *before* your appointments to get used to the language, the tempo of life and the different ways of doing things. You'll find it a worthwhile investment and you should be able to convince your company of this. Talk the situation over with your family and explain the importance of taking those extra days. Discuss how, as a family, you can make up the time with them so you can all benefit by it.

Be curious about your customers' way of life, and don't be afraid to ask questions. In most countries, unlike Sweden, questions are not considered 'nosey'. Provided you ask the right questions at the right time – and that in itself is a skill – you will be showing that you care. If you are to be sent out to work in the foreign subsidiary, or on a project for some years, mix with nationals living in Sweden by joining their associations or clubs and making friends. Embassies, consulates, chambers of commerce, trading houses and the Association for Swedes Abroad, are all good 'briefing centres'.

Try to organise a mentor in your host country who can give you tips on how to function well in the workplace, and even brief you on the unwritten rules of social convention. You need a mentor in the home office too to look after your career within the company. He/she can also keep you posted and up-to-date on the changes within the organisation, and within Sweden!

If possible read their local newspapers and listen to their broadcasts. Read books and articles. One of the best ways to understand values, is to read children's books and fables! It is also a good way to learn the language. Knowledge and understanding will help you function better in the market. You do not have to give up being Swedish. On the contrary, you will probably find you have many traits in common with 'the locals' and, in discovering them, will learn to know yourself a lot better!

Personal Relations

Once again, let me stress the importance attached in many cultures to personal relationships. They take time, sometimes years, but without them you may never reach the negotiation table. A Japanese acquaintance was sent by his company to Latin America. He was told to take a year to build up friendships and not to discuss business during that time. He learnt the language, learnt to play the guitar and sing the local songs. The result was, of course, excellent business for his company, built up on friendship and trust.

Keeping in Touch

It may not be your fault that the decision-making process is so slow in your company, but it is your job to hurry it up and keep the customer warm. Easier said than done? Keep in touch. Write letters and use your telephone and fax to keep the customer informed of all moves. If a customer complains, don't put the blame on someone else, take it yourself *and apologise.* He does not give a damn whose fault it is. He wants things put right and *fast.*

According to a survey made by the Rockefeller Corporation of Pittsburgh as to why customers quit buying from their regular suppliers, 68% quit because of an attitude of *indifference* towards the customer – not keeping in touch, remembering birthdays or important celebrations and not making that phone-call.

Personal relationships are a safeguard against faulty production, late deliveries or slow decisions. Customers will have more sympathy for such eventualities if you are on good speaking terms with them. Regular contacts should also be taken to check that the client is satisfied with the goods and to show interest in their sales' methods and progress.

In some countries it is well worth getting to know the boss's secretary as she is often the eyes and ears of the company.

An enquiry should be handled *without delay*. Whatever it is and whether or not you can foresee immediate business resulting from it, you should have the courtesy to reply. By doing so you may well be opening new channels for future business.

Contacts with Subsidiaries

Keep in touch with subsidiaries and inform them of all decisions made affecting them. Inform them in time of any organisational changes, delays in deliveries, or visits from head office. Spend sufficient time with them on your visits so that they have the chance to bring up relevant matters themselves. Encourage them in their work and *show* enthusiasm for it. Give compliments where they are due, even personal ones are appreciated in many cultures. The last time I passed a compliment to a Swedish woman by remarking on her nice dress, she turned around and looked behind her. Unused to receiving such personal attention, she was convinced I was talking about someone else. But she admitted that it made her feel good for the rest of the day. Don't avoid telling them when you are dissatisfied – out with it! It is often far better to put your cards on the table. Come with *constructive proposals,* not *ready-made solutions.*

Negotiating

Negotiation techniques – making agreements, bargaining and signing contracts differ from country to country, even from company to company. Flexibility is the key-word for success. All parties like to feel they have been accommodated in some way. It does not follow that you will make a bad contract just because you have made a few concessions.

In Japan oral agreements form the foundations for written contracts. Negotiators are concerned with building up relationships (process), not with specifying the actual contract (content). After mutual trust has been established, the essential details only are written up allowing both parties the flexibility of making minor adjustments. A modest amount of bargaining is acceptable. The second best offer is presented first. Trading margins, however, are not large. On the contrary, if margins are too wide, they may inflate the initial price beyond credibility.[1] The film 'Doing Business in Japan – Negotiating a Contract' is an excellent illustration of this.[2]

For the Arab, business relationships start from a base of distrust, and a key objective of negotiations is to build up mutual confidence. This process takes *time* and precludes hard selling. You will get nowhere without a flexible timetable. After the establishment of a good relationship, the visitor often finds that price has become a secondary issue and can be introduced at the end of the ritual. The Arabs enjoy driving a hard bargain and it is an integral part of negotiations. However, they also take into account such considerations as provision of human services as well as price.[1]

When both partners in a negotiation are using a second language in which to communicate, do not be afraid to play back their messages to them, or to repeat yours in other words. It is purely a double-check that you are both talking about the same thing.

In many cases it is advisable to negotiate through a local agent – preferably a native of the country. They will save you many a pitfall and make sure that contracts drawn up have taken account of local conditions. Sometimes they can even act as interpreters and smooth over cultural differences.

Interpreting

The role of the interpreter should not be underestimated. He should be fluent in both languages and conversant with the subject under discussion. You should not rely on your customer's interpreter but preferably take your own with you. Don't overwork him, use simple words not idiomatic ones, speak slowly and give him time to translate. Provide him with documentation in advance to give him time to familiarise himself with the subject. When talking through an interpreter, look at the party who is addressed, not at the interpreter. The same applies when listening to the interpreter.

Bribing

When is a gift not a gift and when does it become a bribe? In Japan, to exchange expensive gifts is considered a courtesy. In China, even a company plastic pen is considered a bribe. The Swedish laws forbidding bribery or the acceptance of bribes are so strict that, if

'Place your order with me, and I'll make your dreams come true.'

adhered to they would, and certainly do, exclude you from many export markets. Bribes are an essential part of the negotiation process in many of the poor countries where officials are badly paid. To refuse to accommodate them, is to lose the contract. And this does not only apply to the poorer countries! To bribe or be bribed makes many of you feel uncomfortable, since this is not part of your cultural heritage. Yet if you do not, someone else will ... Your Swedish honesty is likely to be misinterpreted as being naive. Many women buyers have told me of their embarrassment when offered bribes by prospective suppliers. They could be millionaires today – if it were not for their Swedish norms.

Entertaining

Take care of your visitors when they come to Sweden. Many of you do, I know, but too many do not. You know yourself how unpleasant it is to be left alone in a strange city, especially when you do not speak the language. Entertain them in Swedish fashion by all means, but if you do invite foreigners for crayfish or pea soup brief them on the fact that it *is* the main dish! Invite them to your homes and let them meet your families. They will get a much better insight into Swedish culture if you do, and you will probably enjoy much easier relationships afterwards. If your wife is working, have ready-made food sent in and bill your company. If the worst comes to the worst why not invite them to a restaurant for a meal then home for coffee? If company policy does not encourage you to entertain in your home blaming the rigidity of the taxation system, change your job!

If you do the inviting, then pay – don't haggle over the bill and work out how much each person has eaten and drunk! Equally, if others invite you, accept graciously – don't offer to split the bill or try to pay with coupons! I'm aware that this is quite normal behaviour in Sweden, but in most other countries only students get away with it. In others' eyes such behaviour will be decoded as being *mean..* Insofar as drinking habits are concerned, here too it is usual to pay 'your round ' and if you smoke, to offer your cigarettes.

Gifts

Find out the customs for giving and receiving gifts in each country. What is expected of you? Bring souvenirs from Sweden with you as they will always be appreciated. Most companies have selected a certain number of company gifts, often with their name printed discretely on them. That's fine, but do also give something more personal – especially if you are invited to someone's home. Besides it will save you the embarrassment of buying the wrong coloured flowers. Colours mean different things in different countries too. If you are given a gift, should you open it or wait until your guests have gone to do so?

Taboos

When asked, most people claim that there are no taboos in their own countries – only in others! As I said before, it is only when we step outside our own culture that we begin to see just how many there are!

Talking business at lunch is taboo in most countries unless a working lunch has been agreed upon. Talking about money, politics or religion can be in others. Some companies object to being asked about their turnover, or even the number of employees. In their views these matters only concern themselves and the tax authorities. Anyway, most of it is available from your bank contacts. Religion plays a central role in the lives of many cultures. It is intricably linked with their entire business and social lives. This must be respected, as must their religious ceremonies. It is unforgivable to ridicule them or ignore them.

Should you spend an evening drinking with an Arab in Sweden, forget it and above all do not refer to it when you visit him. The rules of Islam are very strict and forbid alcohol in any form.

If you become 'du' with a client during some evening entertainment, do not keep it up next day in the office, unless asked to do so. The only exception to the rule that I have heard of is IKEA. They sell 'Swedishness' and train their locally-employed staff to speak, think and act like Swedes! Even in Austria, France, Germany and Switzerland, employees are taught to say 'du' to their colleagues. They are encouraged to take Swedish lessons and even top managers work in open-plan offices.

Making Language Communicate

A mistake that most of us make is to assume that our cross-cultural communication problems stem only from language differences and that the problem can be resolved by language training.

We must naturally not under-estimate the importance of language. Nobody would argue that a good command of it will open many locked doors. But having a good vocabulary and speaking grammatically is not enough. We must be able to communicate *effectively* and *affectively* with it.

As said before, language is not just *what* you say but *how, when* and even *where* to say it. For instance, if you praise Swedish quality in countries whose reputation for quality products is not the best, they will dislike you for it and will consider you a swank. Not so in countries which have a good reputation for quality. Similarly, if you talk negatively about Sweden, say in China, where the people are taught the importance of being proud of their nation's achievements, you will be despised for it.

In the world of international business there are many and varied unwritten rules of social behaviour concerning the use of small-talk. How much small-talk, what type of small-talk should be used and for how long, before getting down to business discussions.

'Sweden is fantastic'   'Sweden stinks'

As described on page 87, the use of questions is another obstacle. *When* to ask them and *what sort* of questions can be asked? Many of my own clients have admitted that they hate this question-and-answer game and are not in the slightest interested to know about others' families and personal interests. My reply to them is that they are in the wrong job and should not be working internationally!

Your fate of living in a country with a small isolated language leaves you open to attack from all sides. Everyone expects you to speak *their* language and you do not, according to a survey made by the Swedish Trade Council with 378 small and medium-sized companies. English is used by 22% of those exporting to German-speaking countries, by 68% of those exporting to French-speaking countries and 82% to Spanish-speaking countries, 64% to the Eastern block (excluding the former East Germany) and 72% to Russia.[3]

The survey shows that the majority of you use English as your second language, whether or not it is the mother-tongue of your customers. Then you *must* be able to *communicate* with it. Most of you speak English well but you put so little *feeling* into your words. This, as reported, accounts for many misunderstandings. Neither do you make use of your other communication tools such as body talk. It can confirm or contradict your verbal message. I have met some hair-raising examples of managers who are specialists in the technicalities of the language without communicating with it. I dare not think of the bad reputation they can cause for themselves, their company and Sweden! On the other hand, I have had some examples of others with a poor command of the language. They are much more concerned that their message is being understood, communicate with their entire bodies and are quite unafraid of making fools of themselves. I would send them anywhere in the world with their sensitivity and flexibility.

Ideally, you should naturally learn the national language, especially if you have one specific language market. Just as you find it easier to get under the skin of those who speak Swedish and are flattered by their efforts to speak it. A couple of foreign bank directors I met had taken the trouble to learn Swedish. Banks, they explained, all sell standard products on the same terms – money. The only competition they can offer is service. They found that Swedes trusted their judgement more, and were more ready to accept advice when conversing in their own language, plus the fact that they acquired more Swedish customers.

Learning the Cultural Heritage of Language

Have you ever considered how deeply our roots are dug in our language? Imagine working on some project in the desert for 3 years or so without meeting another Swede. Suddenly one looms up in front of you: 'Är du svensk?' (Are you Swedish?) you ask. At home you probably had nothing whatsoever in common with that Swede, but out there you have a very close rapport. You share so much in common – your history, geography, climate, life-style and, above all your language, thinking patterns and values.

Many of our traditions and behaviour patterns are intricably linked to our language. Take the Swedish language, for instance. Those three little words, 'Tack för maten', (Thank you for the meal), are built into your spine. You take them with you wherever you go. Even a well-travelled businessman will probably, consciously or unconsciously, feel ill-at-ease in a new culture until he has ascertained whether an equivalent phrase exists and is expected of him. Equally so, if he finds himself placed at table with the hostess on his right, is he expected to give a 'Tack för maten' speech? In fact, the honoured guest in most Western countries has the hostess on his left!

Indeed to thank for the food, rather than for the enjoyable company or the entire evening, may well be considered out of place and too

'Tack för maten!'

impersonal in another culture where human relationships mean so much. Symbolically, it can be compared with telling an artist that you find his choice of frame *interesting,* when asked how you like the picture which he has taken five years to paint!

In a private home you can always show appreciation by saying something like: 'This is delicious.' But don't stand up, click your glass to obtain silence, clear your throat and make a formal speech about it. Relax and enjoy yourselves instead.

When you meet your hosts next time, 'Tack för senast', literally translated 'Thank you for the last time' may not be quite appropriate! Maybe something like 'When can you come and see us?' would be more appreciated.

One interesting way to become more aware of your own cultural background, your 'Swedishness', is to jot down as many typical Swedish phrases or proverbs as you can. Because whenever you go on overseas assignments your behaviour will be influenced by them, as will your set of values. Let's help you on your way. 'Att tala är silver, men tiga är guld' – (to speak is silver, but silence is golden) is one of your proverbs. How does this affect your behaviour? The Japanese have an excellent proverb which describes their behaviour: 'The nail that stands up should be hammered down.' In my most provocative moments, I have often described the Swedes as 'The Japanese of the North.' They do, in fact, share some common values.

Making Use of Five Senses

All of you working internationally should make much better use of *all* of your senses. How many of you use your ears to *really* listen and keep tuned-in – not just to the words being spoken, but what lies behind them? The tone in which they are spoken often speaks louder than words and it takes training to de-code the message correctly. How many of you use your eyes to perceive the many silent signals being transmitted, or for that matter are aware of your own? Train your other senses too and learn to use them to communicate and receive hidden messages. As we have seen on pages 81–102, language, tone of voice, silence, gestures, facial expression and eye contact, smell and touch, the conception of space and time and even physical appearance all help to communicate attitudes and impressions. We must be more sensitive for, and to, them. If you are conscious of the fact that you lack the ability to show your emotions, either verbally or non-verbally, don't develop a complex about it and give up. Work on it. Neither Björn Borg nor Ingemar Stenmark could be described as emotional people, yet they are globally admired and respected, and so can you be in your own field.

Translating and Adapting Written Material

Whether or not you speak a language perfectly, it is of the utmost importance that product descriptions, sales brochures and pamphlets should be written in the language of each respective market. Although your agent or customer may read English, the final consumer may not. Those companies lacking this ability should make use of their own subsidiaries, agents, Swedish Trade Offices, or local translation services. They have the ability, not just to translate, but to adapt the content to the market place.

The same applies to advertising. Most Swedish advertising agencies have affiliates in other countries to ensure that the message is adapted to their markets. So make use of your agency's local representatives.

In some countries a notice about your company in their newspapers' editorial column has more effect than an advertisement. Trade magazines are interested in product news too. All the larger news agencies such as Reuters, AP, DPA, UPI, UNS, AFP and Tass are represented in Stockholm and most of the important newspapers have correspondents too. There are also organisations which specialise in providing the foreign mass-media with news material on Swedish products. These include Svensk-Internationella Pressbyrån (SIP), Eibis International and Industrial News Service (INS).

Selling Sweden

One of the biggest problems for a little country of 8 million inhabitants, geographically and linguistically isolated from the rest of the world, is to market itself. To market itself appropriately according to the local conditions applying in the different parts of the world. That costs money, but it is of vital importance if our trading partners are to have confidence in us. Can we really rely on such a little, insignificant country to be able to produce the products we need, in the quantities we require?

Budgets are made available to such bodies as The Swedish Institute, The Swedish Trade Council and The National Central Bureau of Statistics but it is by no means sufficient to produce market-orientated information. Documents, reports and films are made, but the target group is *the world*. Some of the material produced is quite informative but the budget does not stretch to distributing it. So comparatively few people know about it!

When representing your company abroad, you are acting ambassadors for Sweden. As such you must be able to discuss Swedish topical events which have been reported in the international press. The Swedish Institute's Fact Sheets and Current Sweden series take up such subjects. By reading the material available, not just will you be able to answer questions more intelligently, you will be able to compare conditions in Sweden with those prevailing in other countries. Since the material is available in many languages, it will also help you build up your vocabulary. When laws are passed such as MBL you can learn that the English for it is Co-Determination and so on.

For some companies it is advantageous for them to sell their products and services by waving the Swedish flag. By joining missions or participating in the official Swedish stands at exhibitions. Others prefer to 'go it alone', or to play down the Swedish side, dependent often upon the protectionist policy of the country concerned. It is not always a question of reducing costs, but again of cultural awareness.

Qualifications for an International Manager

A manager may have excellent qualifications to carry out his job successfully at home, but these very same qualifications may not endear him on the overseas market. His exceptional drive, for instance, may alienate many of his colleagues and customers who represent cultures in which an individual winner is regarded as having offended all those who lost. Whereas in others, his reticent approach may be scorned. The successful manager must be a cosmopolitan, aware of these differences in behaviour patterns and flexible enough to adapt to them.

According to a Canadian study by Rubin et al based on Canadians working in developing countries around the world, the essential qualifications for an international manager are:

Two-Way Communication: The ability to engage in meaningful dialogue rather than 'lecturing to individuals from the foreign culture'.

Empathy: The ability to see a situation from the other person's perspective.

Respect: The ability to communicate esteem for persons from other cultures.

Personal Knowledge Orientation: The ability to be subjective; to personalise one's knowledge and perception without being judgemental.

Openness: The willingness and ability to share aspects of one's personal life with members of a foreign culture.

Role Integration: The ability to simultaneously emphasise task and relationship dimensions in working with members of a foreign culture.

Tolerance for Ambiguity: The ability to live and work effectively in highly uncertain and unclear cross-cultural situations.

Persistence: The ability to continue to work for a desired goal even in the face of numerous set backs. To approach goal attainment from an equifinality perspective – i.e. that there is more than one best way to reach a goal.[4]

In markets where wisdom comes with age, the Swedish manager's youth may be against him too, and he must learn to adopt a more respectful attitude to his elders.

Age means wisdom and should be respected.

Women – an Untapped Resource

Why are there so few women employed in international management positions? More Swedish women go out to work than any other Western European country and yet they rarely reach management positions. Could it be due to the fact that they have no help in the home to allow them the luxury of self-development in their careers? They have to choose between career and family, and most choose family. It is interesting to discuss these matters with women managers in Third World countries, comparatively many of whom have reached top positions. They have chauffeurs, private secretaries, housekeepers, cooks, maids, nannies and gardeners to be able to cope. But I suppose that is not 'the Swedish Way' to let others do your dirty work? So what is the solution? Much interest has been shown recently in Sweden by both the public and private sectors to giving men and women equal rights on the labour market. Here is an area where Sweden could be a pioneer by carefully selecting competent women to wave the Swedish flag. Take a look too at the list of essential qualifications for an international manager on page 127. Don't women fit the job description, sometimes better even than men?

Foreigners – an Untapped Resource

Although Swedish multinational companies mainly employ local managing directors in their foreign subsidiaries, they are rarely represented on their boards. In fact, the situation has not changed much since this book came out 10 years ago, in spite of the internationalisation process which has taken place! Only a handful of foreigners are, in fact, represented at board level. Why is this?

For a little country, Sweden has an astounding number of very large companies. Many of them claim that they are 'international' – not 'Swedish'. Yet, with a purely Swedish management, they can hardly do otherwise than live up to their reputation of 'globalising, the Swedish way.'

Has the fact that they have been so successful in the past on world markets, lured them into complacency? That Swedish industry is well aware of the importance of internationalisation, there is no doubt. Their mergers and acquisitions on EC markets is proof enough of this. Don't they realise how much they are losing by not promoting foreigners to their management boards? The resource that they bring with them from their cultural backgrounds and markets is invaluable, and one of the only unique resources with which companies today have to compete.

I have participated in many sessions on this subject with companies. Their excuse is usually that the Swedish taxation system does not motivate foreign managers to work in Sweden. Also that they do not understand the Swedish system and Swedish ways! But *you* do! They can be the bridge between your cultures and even broaden your horizons on other markets.

Cross-Cultural Awareness Training

The importance and acceptance of cross-cultural training as an integral part of management development is slowly being recognised. But there is still a long way to go. Most Swedish companies today either sell to or buy from foreign markets; are engaged in transnational joint-ventures, mergers or acquisitions; participate in international projects or employ foreign workers.

Then there are all the subsidiaries of foreign companies in Sweden who need to be briefed on 'the Swedish way' in order to function better and quicker. The foreign workers on the shop-floor need it, to understand one another and their Swedish colleagues better. The Swedish workers need it to broaden their horizons and be more understanding of the problems of adapting to the Swedish way of life.

The receptionists, telephonists, secretaries and administrative staff need it to be able to receive and communicate with foreign visitors appropriately. The service engineers, with the world as their market, need it. As do all technicians and staff who work with and train their overseas colleagues. Those involved with project management, production and marketing need it too.

Not forgetting those 'mobile families' who are sent out on 3-5 year contracts. For them, the family support is essential. If they are unhappy with the posting, the expatriate manager will not be able to function properly at work. It is not too easy to recruit staff in Sweden for long-term postings when the family is dependent upon two incomes. The spouse (99% the wife) is not guaranteed to get her job back on her return to Sweden, and she also loses her pension points.

15 years ago, I sat in a discussion on these subjects with a group who was preparing a Bill for Parliament to enforce a security plan for accompanying spouses. The discussion is still taking place. However, a little light is shining at the end of the tunnel. Soon, hopefully, it will be the wives who will also be offered the overseas postings. Then, I feel assured, a Bill will be enforced to see that the accompanying *men* don't lose out!

The need for both pre-departure training, on location assistance and preparation for their re-entry to Sweden is indisputable. Some companies encourage spouses to pay a visit to the country concerned to help them look for accommodation. Others expect families to live for months in hotels while trying to find suitable accommodation.

And, last but not least, Swedish foreign subsidiaries need it. Indeed, it is here that multinationals have shown increased awareness of the importance of holding regular get-togethers with their foreign subsidiaries. Previously, these meetings were purely technical, one-way information, to keep subsidiaries informed of company developments. But today, more and more time is given in the programme to checking on and improving HQ-subsidiary relationships, and to defining common goals and values.

Technical knowledge alone is not enough today in our competitive world.

As I claimed in the introduction, prior to any training, companies should carry out a cultural analysis, or cultural mapping. Only then can they can get a full picture of the company culture and its training needs, and take into account all the resources available to them within their own companies.

A few of the larger companies have set up special departments for coping with family expatriation. Even fewer help with repatriation which has proved to be more of a problem! In my 17 years' experience of working in the field, it is those companies who set up their *own* 'briefing centres', using their *own* internal resources, together with the support of a cross-cultural trainer, who can best equip their staff to function well on 'their markets'.

More qualified use should be made of the foreigners resident in Sweden to train cultural awareness. According to studies made, roughly every fifth refugee who comes to Sweden has an university education. But these engineers and professors cannot find jobs within their professions. Instead, they are sorting post, working in hospitals or as ticket collectors on tube stations. What a waste of resource! Companies could use them, not just for their technical competence, but even as cultural experts of their nations. Preferably they should be foreigners who speak Swedish because they understand better the cultural aspects and have themselves experienced the communication problems involved.

Training can be done in different ways but let me give an example of one of my own training programmes. I call it my 'luxury' programme, as I only accept five or ten people on the course so I may work individually with them. If managers are to train to project their personalities in accordance with the business and social practices prevailing in their markets, they must be trained individually.

It covers 3 stages:

Cultural self-awareness. To discover the unique qualifications which you bring to your work, based on your own background.

Cross-cultural awareness. To discover those similarities and differences in others' behaviour which can synergise or conflict with your own.

Cross-cultural skills. To discover and develop your own personal skills, including language, which will enable you to communicate more effectively and affectively on your markets.

We start by looking at ourselves and finding the answers to such questions as:

What sort of impression do I personally make on my foreign contacts?

Why are there so many misunderstandings about Sweden and the Swedes?

Then we go on to:

How can I learn to understand and work efficiently with people with different customs, values and behaviour?

How can such differences affect a negotiation?

Secretaries, Telefax and Telephone Operators

More training is needed for all these people. Especially as most of you rely on them to produce your English texts and messages for you! They do a good job but you expect too much of them. Few of them have had any business training and consequently do not master the business language. I have seen many shocking examples of un-businesslike letters. If I draw attention to them I am told: 'My secretary wrote it and she has lived a year in the States.' Would that make *your* English perfect?

I am convinced that it is lack of confidence in your own ability to dictate letters in foreign languages and in your secretary's to correct them, which explains your reticence to reply to letters. But this does not excuse it. Both of you need training.

Many foreigners object to being faxed when a letter would be more polite. A fax should be used to pass quick information, but never to replace a 'thank-you' letter nor to apologise for short-comings.

Use of the telephone is another aspect which gets overlooked so far as training is concerned. It costs nothing to answer the phone in a friendly voice, preferably with both names – 'Per Svensson'. If you are busy, ask politely if you could take their number and call back instead of scaring them out of their wits. Your telephonists need training too in this respect. They should not leave callers hanging on the line without coming back to give them a report of the situation. As reported, since flexible office hours were made official, this is an all-too-frequent occurence. They should be informed what time you are expected in so they can tell the caller at once and not just cut him off when nobody answers your phone. Sweden is the land of 'telephonitus'. It is comparatively cheap and Swedes use it accordingly. Others avoid it – at all cost! Sweden has more telephones per capita than almost any other country in the world.

Some foreigners dislike to be telephoned by your secretary and to have messages passed through her. You can't blame *her* for not being aware of the hierarchical prestige prevailing in the different countries, but *you* should be. Are your customers so inferior that you can pass them off on your secretary? Because that is how you make them feel. Do you consider yourself so important and your time so valuable that you can't do it yourself? This is how your effectivity is interpreted by them.

It is often the secretaries, receptionists and telephonists who have the first contacts with prospective customers and who are left to cope with irate ones, due to your impolite, sometimes insulting behaviour. They create an image of your company and should be given every support and incentive to do a good job. No money should be spared on their training.

Conclusion

Jean Monet, the founding father of the European Community, is quoted as saying: 'If I had to start again the challenge to integrate Europe, I would probably start with culture.'

Once again, it is *people,* influenced by their country of origin, who determine what actions they will take – whether we are talking world affairs, politics or trade. If we are to remain competitive as a nation, or business, we need to be aware of the different influences in peoples' lives which account for their actions.

Multinational companies need to learn to analyse and recognise the cultural differences prevailing within their organisations in order to benefit from them. Only then can they build their competitive strength on the unique resources of the cultural mix within their organisations.

The last years' global events have taught us the importance of being well-informed, of understanding others' minds, and of building and maintaining relationships – even in times of crisis. Relationships take time, but it is time well spent.

As said in the introduction, people are judged by the impressions they make. It becomes unimportant then to discuss whether they are facts, myths or caused by the communication complex. But that something should be done, there is no doubt. It is up to all of you who have read this far to see where the cap fits and improve your own communication skills. So CHEER UP AND START COMMUNICATING, or remember that, in the words of Ella Wheeler-Wilcox: 'Laugh and the world laughs with you. Cry and you cry alone.'

8 Advice to Foreigners

Businessmen

So you have been smirking and nodding wisely while devouring these pages. But now it's your turn! Have you ever tried to understand what makes the Swede tick? Did you ever try to dig beneath the shell and so develop a more worthwhile relationship? You can't afford the time? That's up to you, but if you are selling or intend to enter the Swedish market, you must.

Many of you have done so. You told me about it and agreed that it paid off. Some of you went to the other extreme and learnt Swedish. Then *you* experienced the difficulties of projecting your true personality in a foreign language. You learnt then how unrewarding it is to judge from first impressions and how misinterpreted they can be. You learnt that behind an unfriendly face and an aggressive tone may lie a basically kind, friendly human being. Just as sensitive as you or I – probably more so. But his culture inhibits him from showing his feelings, so they are all pent up inside. That is why he has difficulties to express his enthusiasm for your propositions, or distaste of them. And why he rarely enjoys a good belly-laugh in public places.

As individuals, they may give the impression of having few controversial things to say. But believe me, when you get to know them, they are just as argumentative and critical as you are. The difference is that they rarely criticise each other – not face-to-face anyway! By not doing so, they suffer from the illusion that they are kinder to each other than you are. Should someone dare to criticise their point of view in public, they are inclined to take it personally.

The attitude which you so often mistakenly interpret as indifference is, in fact, their way of showing consideration for you as a human being. Assuming that you react the same way, they keep quiet rather than risk hurting your feelings.

If you wish to do business in Sweden, you should highlight the technical aspects of your product. They want to know all the facts and the direct benefits. An essential is to have your products tested in Sweden before trying to market them.

Their reticence in answering letters stems, I am convinced, from their perfectionism. They hate to be caught out making grammatical mistakes. Why not suggest that they just mark their reply in telegraphic style on your enquiry, and fax it back to you?

Their aversion to conflict and their efforts to avoid confrontations can cause problems and delays. Use your sixth sense – if you sense that there are differences of opinion, clear them up at once. No decision will be taken until they are.

Don't cut in on a Swede when he is talking, or finish his sentences for him. This will only fluster him and you may never get to the root of the problem. Slow down your tempo, if necessary, and learn to relax and be patient. Swedes are comfortable with silence. They use it to digest your questions, formulate their reply and to motivate their next move, so bear with them. You may even learn to appreciate it too! However curious they are about you, they will rarely ask *personal* questions, but they will be more than happy to listen if you want to open up. They have a strong sense of privacy and don't wish to intrude on yours.

Although the Swedes are a rather homogeneous people, it is difficult to generalise about them. They will forgive me for so-doing, I know, because they are generous that way. As with all nations – but maybe less so than most – you have rich and poor, educated and less educated, town and country people. If you come from a class-conscious country, you will probably try to find your 'rightful place' within the society. This is no easy task since the usual outward symbols such as accent, schools, accessibility to those in powerful positions, material possessions, 'the right side of town' and so on are, officially, available to all.

They are a strange mixture of formality and informality. 30 years ago they addressed each other by titles and spoke in the third person. Some of them still think in that way, even if they have adopted the informal 'du'. Accordingly when addressing a foreigner they take great pains not to offend in this respect and try to avoid any personal reference to you. You can help by making it clear from the start that you like to be known as Bill or Mr. X. This applies particularly to you Americans working here for multinationals. Your colleagues are loathe to be too familiar with you. You always address them by their first names and that is fine, but does not necessarily mean that you intend them to do likewise. So make it clear to them how you would like them to address you and save them that embarrassment.

To get to know a Swede, you need to go more than 50% of the way to meet him. Don't give up after the first try, but don't push too hard – you can scare him off too! Give him time and you will find he reacts to openness and an easy manner. He admires these traits in others and will become your friend for life. Don't take it personally if he doesn't invite you home. It's probably against company policy, or he doesn't want to put his working wife to the trouble.

Due to the combination of high taxes and living conditions, families need the two incomes. More Swedish wives go out to work than in any other Western European country. Another reason is that the Swedes are very house-proud and wouldn't dream of inviting you home if they haven't had the time to spring-clean, do the shopping and cook a 3-course meal. If they have young children, they will have to be fetched from day-care-centres, fed, bathed and put to bed before you arrive. All this after a hard day's work! So you can understand that by the time they have coped, they are exhausted and the evening has gone. If you really want to get to know the Swedish way of do-it-yourself living, invite yourself and stress that you would enjoy to help with these chores - if you really would! Take with you your tax-free allowance, and inform your Swedish hosts in advance so they can avoid the time and expense of queuing at the State Monopoly.

You have to be prepared to do-it-yourself in Sweden. That means carrying your own baggage, pressing your own trousers and skirts at hotels, cleaning your own shoes, etc. Due to exorbitant labour costs, these services are provided for you in the rooms, even in the more expensive hotels.

Similarly, few people have servants in Sweden. If they do, it is certainly nothing to swank about – on the contrary! So they do their own cooking, scrup their own floors, clean their own windows and mow their own lawns. You will appreciate, therefore, that the Swede has to divide his time carefully between his work and home. Accordingly, with his long vacations and flexibile working hours he is probably, in foreign eyes, often absent from his office.

Ordinary office hours are 8 a.m. to 4.30 p.m. and no Saturdays. However, flexible working hours allow employees to start their day as early as 7 a.m. and leave by 3 p.m. The whole country practically closes down during July when the industrial holidays take place. Forget about making appointments on Friday afternoons. You will probably be told that your contact is in a meeting when he in fact left early to make the most of the weekend. You should be aware of doing business in Sweden during the period between Christmas and 6th January, and over Easter. May is a tricky month too, with several bank holidays coming on top of each other.

So pick your months carefully, but if you intend to mix business with pleasure and sight-seeing, those are the times! As one of our well-respected industrialists advised:

Try to get on such friendly terms with your business contacts and their families that they will invite you to their 'stuga' (log cabin) while you are here. Bring your bathing gear, your golf clubs and a pair of yachting shoes. If you are invited under such

conditions you will find a new breed of Swedish businessman –
calmer, more thoughtful, able to take long-term views without
being disturbed by the telephone, and apt to brainstorm and
philosophise during the light summer evenings over several
whisky-sodas.

Let's face it, despite all our complaints and frustrations with Sweden and the Swedes, they've got something very special here which gets under our skins. Otherwise, why do so many of us who were passing through, stay on and miss it so much when we leave? Be careful, you may get caught too, but in the meantime, good luck!

Immigrants[1]

So you have decided to come to Sweden and make your home here, at least for the time being.

You have to be prepared for any number of surprises – some of them pleasant, others less so. A culture shock is inevitable. My advice to you all is: try to adjust to life in Sweden, but do not lose sight of your own identity, since you have a lot from your own culture with which to enrich the Swedish society.

Language is an important part of a country's culture and, without it, you can never participate in that culture. I wondered myself why I should bother to learn the language of some 8 million people when I had no intention of staying here. But it wasn't until I had learnt Swedish, that I began to understand and respect values, attitudes, customs and habits around me. Doors that had previously been closed, now opened. I found it easier to understand and interpret signals, facial expressions, gestures and silence – and to get work!

So my advice to you is to learn Swedish as quickly as possible. Try not to condemn or judge anything before you have learnt to under-stand the language. If you have brought your family with you, your children will learn Swedish at school. Do not make them your interpreters. Take a Swedish course yourself and make certain your spouse does too, to avoid isolation in the home.

It is natural that you should get advice from fellow countrymen already living here. It gives you a feeling of security being together with people who speak your own language and who share your values and customs. They can help you understand and adjust to life in Sweden. But a word of warning is necessary.

Many of your fellow countrymen may themselves be suffering from culture shock, which means that they may either be very critical of the Swedish society or else, on the contrary, have gone native and see Sweden through rose-tinted spectacles. In both cases, you will be seeing Sweden through their eyes and probably be influenced by them. So try to get to know Sweden and make friends with the Swedes yourself.

You will certainly not be able to go about this in the same way as you do at home because things are different here. Every country has its unwritten laws about ways of getting to know people. Because of the climate and expense, few Swedes have the habit of sitting down at a pavement café, dropping in to their local pub, or simply meeting in the square to hob-nob. Yet they love outdoor sports such as jogging, walking in the woods, orienteering, bird-watching, taking advantage of the 'allemänsrätt' – the freedom to walk, picnic, pick mushrooms and berries anywhere – boating and all usual athletic sports. Make one of these very Swedish activities your hobby, and join a local club or association.

Swedes do not usually drop in on one another, at least not in the towns and cities. They hate to intrude and respect each other's privacy. For this reason they often have little contact with their neighbours. You can try inviting your Swedish neighbours in for coffee, for your national dish or to your national club. But don't be offended if they make excuses. Just try again another time when they have got used to seeing you around.

Again, do not take it personally if they don't return your invitation. They are not accustomed to asking you to 'drop in' and, to issue a formal invitation, would involve them in lots of work. (See Advice to Businessmen).

Many of you come from countries where smiles are an important, though perhaps unconscious, part of your social pattern. The Swedes are hardly likely to win any prizes for smiling, but they admire those who do and respond, discreetly, to it. So carry on smiling!

So get to know the Swedes and build your own life-style to bridge the two cultures. This does *not* mean that you have to become just like Swedes and lose your own identity. On the contrary, there are certain values and life-styles which you will be able to accept and which complement your own. Others, not so. Never forget how much you have to give to Sweden and its people just because you are the unique person you are – a product of your own culture.

Good luck to you!

Reference List

Introduction
1 *Hur djupt sitter svenskheten?* Forskning och Framsteg (6/86) Åke Daun & Jean Phillips-Martinsson.

Chapter 1
1 *Svensk mentalitet,* Rabén & Sjögren. (1989) Åke Daun.

Chapter 3
1 Name given in Sweden to those people internationally known as Turkish Armenians.

2 Background material extracted from the Swedish Institute's Fact Sheets and Current Sweden series.

3 *Trends in alcohol and drug use in Sweden.* The Swedish Council for Information on Alcohol and other Drugs. (Report 89).

4 *Scandinavians – that's us!* p. 8–9. Willy Breinholst.

5 Employment Conditions Abroad, 15 Britten St., London.

6 All statistics quoted in this chapter where provided by the Swedish National Bureau of Statistics, unless otherwise stated.

7 *Sweden Now* and *Dagens Industri.* (1980).

Chapter 5
1 *Introduction to Kinesics,* University of Lousville (1952), R. L. Birdwhistell.

2 *Manwatching* (1978) Jonathan Cape London, Desmond Morris.

3 *Culturgram Communication Aid* (1990) and *Building Bridges of Understanding* (1979) Brigham Young University.

4 *Manwatching* (1978) and *Gestures* (1979) Jonathan Cape, London. Desmond Morris.

5 *The Hidden Dimension* (1966) Edward T. Hall.

6 *Personal Space* (1969), Robert Sommer.

7 *The Silent Language in Overseas Business* Havard Business Review (May–June, 1960). E. T. Hall.

Chapter 6

1 *Culture's Consequences.* (Abridged version) Sage Publications. (1984) Geert Hofstede Motivation, Leadership and Organization: *Do American Theories Apply Abroad?* Organizational Dynamics (1980). Geert Hofstede.

2 *The Cultural Diversity of Western Conceptions of Management.* (Feb.1987) André Laurant.

3 *Managing Relationships with Foreign Subsidiaries.* Sveriges Mekanförbund (1984) Gunnar Hedlund & Per Åman.

4 *An Anglo-Swedish Culture Clash.* Eurobusiness (Nov. 1990) Robert Brown & Jean Phillips-Martinsson.

5 FA-Rådet (1987 unpublished).

6 *How To Do Buisness with a Frenchman.* Harper's Magazine Aug. 1965. E. Russel Eggers.

Chapter 7

1 *Business Customs and Protocol* (1987) SRI, Klaus D. Schmidt.

2 *Doing Business in Japan – Negotiating a Contract.* (1979) Vision.

3 *Företag och Språk* Swedish Trade Council (1980).

4 *Women as Androgynous Managers* (1979) Nancy J. Adler

Chapter 8

1 *A General Introduction for Immigrants.* (1983) Statens Invandrarverk Jean Phillips-Martinsson. Sweden.

Literature List

Adams, P. *Language in Thinking*. The Chaucer Press Ltd 1972.

Adler, N. J. *International Dimensions of Organizational Behaviour*. The Kent International Business Series. (1986).

Adler, N. J. *Women as Androgynous Managers*. Graduate School of Management. Univ'y of California. L. A. 1979.

Adler, N. J. & Izraeli N. *Women in Management Worldwide*, M. E. Sharpe, 1988.

Argyle, M. *Social Encounters*. Penguin Books. 1973. *Social Interaction*. Methuen & Co Ltd. 1969. *Bodily Communication*. Methuen & Co Ltd. 1975.

Austin, Paul Britten. *On Being Swedish*. Secker & Warburg Ltd. 1968.

Birdwhistell, R. L. *Introduction to Kinesics*. University of Louisville, Kentucky. 1952.

Breinholst, W. *Scandinavians – that's us*.

Brigham Young University. *Building Bridges of Understanding 1979. Culturgrams,* Language and Intercultural Research Center, 1990.

Brown R. & Phillips-Martinsson J. *An Anglo-Swedish Culture Clash*. Eurobusiness (Nov. 1990).

Casse P. *Training for the Cross-Cultural Mind*, SIETAR, 1979.

Casse P. *Training for the Multicultural Manager*, SIETAR, 1982.

Casse P. & Deol S. *Managing Intercultural Negotiations,* SIETAR, 1985.

Condon, John C, Yousef, Fathi. *An Introduction to Intercultural Communication*. Bobbs-Merrill Education Publishing, Indianapolis. 1975.

Cook, M. *Interpersonal Perception*. Penguin Books. 1971.

Daun, Åke & Phillips-Martinsson, J. *Forskning och Framsteg* (Nr. 6/86).

Daun, Å. *Svensk mentalitet*. Rabén & Sjögren. 1989.

Davis, F. *Inside Intuition*. New America Library. 1975.

Ekman P., and Friesen, W. V. *Emotion in the Human Face*. Pergamon Press, New York. 1972.

Evans P., Dos Y., Laurant A. *Human Resource Management in International Firms*. An Insead report.

Farb P. *What Happens When People Talk*. Jonathan Cape. 1974.

Fast J. *Body Language*. Souvenir Press Ltd. 1971.

Fisher G. *Mindsets*, Intercultural Press, Yarmouth 1988.

Fisher G. *International Negotiation*, Intercultural Press, Yarmouth 1980.

Fisher R & Ury W. *Getting to Yes*, Houghton Mifflin Co. Boston.

Fisher R. and Brown S. *Getting Together*, Houghton Mifflin Co. Boston, 1988.

Goffman, E. *Presentation of Self in Everyday Life*. N. Y. Anchor. 1959. *Relations in Public*. Harper Colophon Books Ltd. 1972. *Encounters*. Penguin University Books. 1961.

Hall, E. T. *The Hidden Dimension*. Garden City: Doubleday. 1966.

Hall, E. T. *The Silent Language in Overseas Business*. May/June, 1960. Havard Business Review.

Hall, E. T. *The Silent Language*. Doubleday. New York.1959.

Hall, E. T. *Beyond Culture*. Garden City: Anchor-Doubleday. 1976.

Hall, E. T. *The Dance of Life,* Anchor-Doubleday.

Hall, E. T. *Understanding Cultural Differences,* Intercultural Press, Yarmouth 1989.

Hall, E. T. and Mildred Reed Hall. *Understanding Cultural Differences Germans, French, Americans.* Intercultural Press, Yarmouth 1990.

Hardin, S & Phillips, D (Ed) *Contrasting Values in Western Europe.* Studies in Modern Society. MacMillan, London 1986.

Harris, Philip R., Moran, Robert T. *Managing Cultural Differences.* Gulf Publishing Co, Houston, Texas. 1979.

Harris, Thomas A. *I'm OK – You're OK.* Pan, London & Sydney.

Hastorf, A. H., Schneider, D. J., Polefka, J. *Person Perception.* Addison-Wesley. 1979.

Hedlund G. & Åman P. *Managing Relationships with Foreign Subsidiaries,* Sveriges Mekanförbund (1984).

Herlitz G. *Kulturgrammatik.* Konsultförlaget 1989.

Hofstede G. *Culture's Consequences,* Sage Publications 1980 (Abridged version, 1984).

Hofstede G. *Motivation, Leadership and Organization: Do American Theories Apply Abroad?* Organizational Dynamics.

Hofstede G. *Cultures & Organizations: Software of the Mind.* Mc Graw-Hill, UK (1991).

Jenkins, D. *The Progress Machine.* Low and Brydone (Printers) Ltd, London. 1968.

Joint, P. and Warner. M. *Managing in Different Cultures.* Universitetsförlaget 1985.

Knapp, M. L. *Noverbal Communication in Human Interaction.* N. Y. Holt, Rinehart & Winston. 1972.

Kohls, L. Robert. *A Survival Kit for Overseas Living*. Intercultural Network/Systran Publications. Chicago, Illinois. 1984.

Kohls. L. Robert. *Developing Intercultural Awarenss* SIETAR (1981).

Laine-Sveiby, K. *Svenskhet som strategi*. Timbro. 1987.

Laurant A. *The Cultural Diversity of Western Conceptions of Management*. International Studies of Management and Organisation Vol XIII (1/2) p. 75–96.

Laurant B. *12 familjer i EG berättar*, SAF 1991.

Laver, John & Hutcheson, Sandy. *Communication in Face to Face Interaction*. Penguin Books Ltd. 1972.

Lohmann, Hans. *Psykisk Hälsa och Mänsklig Miljö*. Socialstyrelsen. 1973.

Mehrabian, A. *Silent Messages* Belmont Calif., Wadsworth. 1971.

Mole J. *Mind Your Manners*, The Industrial Society 1990.

Morris, D. *Manwatching*. Jonathan Cape/Elsevier, London/Oxford. 1978. *Gestures*. Jonathan Cape/London. 1979.

Morris, Desmond. *The Naked Ape*. Jonathan Cape, London. 1967.

Nierenberg, Gerald I., & Calero, Henry H. *How to Read a Person Like a Book*. Pocket Books, N. Y. 1973. *Meta-Talk. The Guide to Hidden Meanings in Conversation*. Cornerstone Library. N. Y. 1973.

Nierenberg, Gerald I. *Fundamentals of Negotiating*. Hawthorn Books Inc. 1968.

Phillips-Martinsson, J. *Cross-Cultural Relations in International Marketing*. 1979.

Phillips-Martinsson, J. *Språk, kommunikation och kultur i internationell marknadsföring*. Exporthandboken 1982, Exportrådet.

Phillips. Martinsson J. *A General Introduction for Immigrants.* Statens Invandrarverk (1983).

Rhinesmith, Stephen H. *Bring Home the World.* AMACOMM (div. of American Management Associations, N. Y.) 1975.

Scheflen, A. E. and Ashcroft, N. *Human Territories.* Englewood Cliffs, N. J. Prentice Hall. 1976.

Scheflen, A. E. *How Behaviour Means.* Gordon and Breach, New York. 1973.

Schmidt, Klaus D. *SRI International 'Business Customs and Protocol' series.* (1987).

Scott B. *The Skills of Negotiating,* Gower, 1987.

Sommer, R. *Personal Space. N. J. Prentice Hall.*

Swedish Institute. Fact Sheets and *'Current Sweden'* series.

Swedish Trade Council. 'Företag och Språk.' 1980.

Torbiörn, Ingemar. *Att Leva Utomlands.* S N S 1976.

Weinskall, Theodore, D. *Culture and Management.* Penguin Books. 1977.

Wylie, L. *Organizational Behaviour of the French School of Jacques Lecoq.*

Videos/Films

Doing Business in Japan Negotiating a Contract, Vision New York, 1979.

Going International Series of fourteen 30-min films and videos. Copeland Griggs Productions (Can be ordered through the Intercultural Press, Inc. PO Box 700, Yarmouth, Maine, USA).

All Scandinavian orders for Intercultural Press publications can be ordered through Global Kommunikasjon A.S., Eplerod N-3080 Homestrand, Norway.